Salmon River Legends

and
CAMPFIRE CUISINE

by Darcy Williamson
Steven Shephard

illustrated by Shannon Dee

— A Maverick Publication —

— First Edition —

Maverick Publications
Drawer 5007 • Bend, Oregon 97708

Contents

Illustrations

Introduction

"The Salmon River? That's somewhere out west, right?" was the reaction I got when I told friends I was going white water rafting. In truth I didn't know exactly where the Salmon River was either until I started doing research on rafting outfitters for my trip.

Surprising as all this may sound, consider that I am a born and bred Easterner working in New York City. My friends and I are not alone here in our admitted fuzziness with the geography of the rest of the country. One of the most famous covers of the *New Yorker* magazine featured a cartoon by Saul Steinberg showing a typical Manhattanite's view of the world. In the foreground, in great detail, were the skyscrapers of the city bounded by a big, blue Hudson River. In the distance, at the horizon, was a brown hump labeled China. The space in between was compressed into thin strips: a green one for the rest of the country and a blue one for the Pacific.

So it was with a great sense of adventure in unknown territory that I made my plans to go to Idaho and explore the Salmon River in a raft. And what an adventure it proved to be! Thanks to the expert arrangements provided by Salmon River Outfitters, the company I chose to guide me down the river, I spent five glorious days floating down an eighty-mile section of the Main Salmon as it flows through the second deepest canyon in the United States, all the while being royally wined and dined by Steven Shephard and his five guides.

I can imagine no better way to explore a river, to really feel it, than by raft. With oars as the only source of power, the senses are free to absorb what the river has to offer: the chilly splash of mountain water as the rafts bend and hurtle through surging rapids, the astringent pungency of pine trees rising up from the banks, the peace of long stretches of calm water interrupted by the calls of canyon wrens and the roar of approaching rapids, the beauty of grass covered hills glowing golden in twilight, the flavor, or rather the clear and wonderful lack thereof in the water that tumbles from the many feeder creeks into the Salmon.

Getting to the Salmon River was an adventure in itself. I flew first to Boise, the capital of Idaho, where I boarded a small prop plane to fly northeast across the state to the town of Salmon. The flight was a humbling introduction to Idaho's River of No Return Wilderness, the largest government regulated wilderness area in "the lower forty-eight," through which the Salmon River flows. For about an hour we flew over a seemingly endless mass of craggy, sardine-packed mountain ranges, with little hint of human presence other than an occasional logging road. This was clearly not land made for easy living. Only pioneers and gold-obsessed miners would choose to eek out an existence here.

The town of Salmon couldn't be a more fitting starting point for rafting expeditions on the Main Salmon. It is situated on the banks of its namesake river about thirty miles south of the confluence with the North Fork of the Salmon. The river, as it flows through town, appears to be a pleasant, almost tame current with few, if any, hints of the rapids ahead. A walk down the dusty main street lined with river related businesses and serious bars is like taking a step back in time. Thanks to the absence of developers, it's not hard to imagine the town of Salmon as it must have been when it was the bustling starting point, at the turn of the century, for miners spurred by gold in the Salmon River Canyon and sweepboat operators who dared the rapids in their flat-bottomed wooden boats to supply the miners with equipment.

Although Salmon was our meeting point for outfitter and passengers, the actual rafting didn't begin there. Salmon River Outfitters provided a bus that wound its way on a winding dirt road built precariously at times on the steep banks of the river past such landmarks as Pine Creek Rapids, the sight of which over 150 years earlier had convinced Clark of the Lewis and Clark Expedition to abandon his exploration of the Salmon as a possible route to the Columbia. The road ended at a boat ramp where the rafts were inflated and carefully packed with provisions and equipment. We climbed aboard what would be our self-sufficient homebase for the next five days and headed into the Idaho wilderness.

The Salmon is one of the most popular rivers for rafting in the country today—and no wonder! Besides its well-spaced mix of turbulent rapids and lazy stretches of calm water there are Indian pictographs to be examined, abandoned miners' settlements to be explored, wildlife to be spotted, and natural hot springs to relax in. For me, five days on the Salmon was the minimum I needed to begin to absorb the majesty of the wilderness and lose track of the time so deliberately structured by city life.

My particular trip on the Salmon was made more meaningful with the addition of the author, Darcy Williamson. Being raised in Idaho, Darcy was a font of information on many subjects including food, wildlife, and the American Indian. Darcy augmented the legends the guides told with stories of her own. Wherever we hiked along the river bank she pointed out various plants the Indians used for food or medicinal purposes. The jumble of bird songs we heard were easily identified by Darcy. Near an abandoned miner's cabin she discovered long forgotten apricot and cherry plum trees laden with ripe, extraordinarily flavorful fruit. Suffice to say that no time spent with Darcy was boring.

This book is a natural outgrowth of Darcy's love of Idaho and her menu and food preparation for Steven Shephard's Salmon River Outfitters. It is a treasure of information for those fortunate enough to float down the Salmon and an entertaining insight for those who are not!

by Kempy Minifie

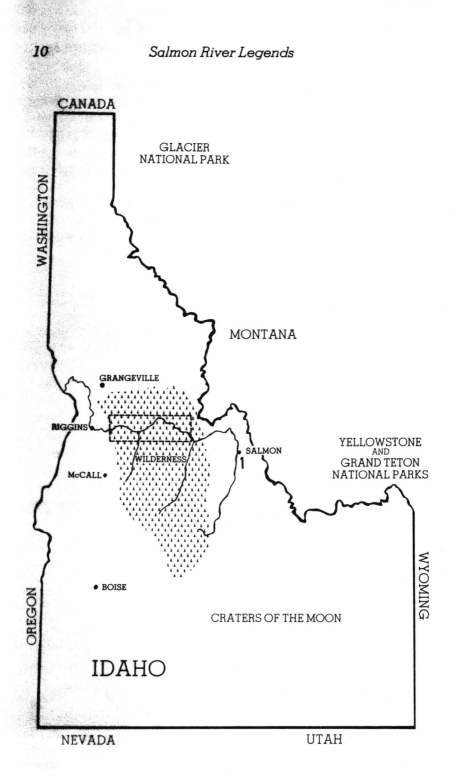

The Founding of Salmon, Idaho

In 1866, a group of former Confederate soldiers from Virginia, Georgia and the Carolinas started prospecting on Napias Creek where it flows into Panther Creek, a tributary of the Salmon. On July 16th, they discovered traces of gold and sunk a shaft to bedrock. They began panning out gold at the rate of one to five dollars a pan.

The Southern prospectors named the site after their hero, Robert E. Lee, calling it Leesburg. Within months the population of Leesburg swelled to 3,000. New camps sprang up, bringing over 7,000 persons to the area. One of the new camps established just up the canyon was started by former Union soldiers and called Grantsville. From time to time feuds erupted between the two camps. The only person killed during one of these skirmishes, however, was an innocent person passing through the area. Eventually the camps merged to become a larger Leesburg. With such rapid growth of the area, supplies became scarcer and scarcer. As a result, Salmon City arose fifteen miles to the southeast, situated at the forks of the Salmon and Lemhi Rivers.

Supplies were brought to Salmon by wagon train from Utah, Washington and Montana, then were packed by a mule to Leesburg. Because of the cost of transporting supplies, flour sold for thirty cents per pound and sugar for eighty cents. Kerosene was known to sell for twenty-five dollars per gallon, since, should it spill in the freight wagon, the food could be ruined.

Colonel George L. Shoup, who had participated in the Indian massacre at Sand Creek, Colorado, helped to lay out Main Street and the two cross streets which became the town's business district. Stoup owned the major mercantile in town and built the three-story brick building that stands at the corner of Main and Center Streets. He was appointed Idaho's last territorial governor and elected the State's first

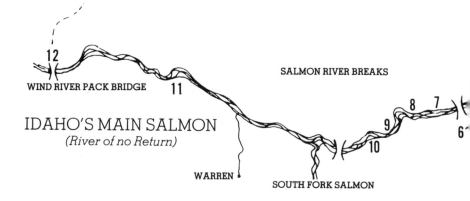

governor. Later he served in the U.S. Senate from 1891-1901.

G.L. Shoup wasn't the first historical figure to occupy the area where the town of Salmon now stands. In 1832 the site at the forks of the two rivers was a winter camp for brigades of the Hudson's Bay Company, the American Fur Company and the Rocky Mountain Fur Company. Jim Bridger, Joe Meek, Henry Fraeb, Tom Fitzpatrick, Kit Carson, Joseph Walker and Captain Bonneville all warmed their hands over campfires at this site.

Four-Eyed Smith and Charlie Williams had a cabin amidst the Salmon River Canyon. They raised a garden—kind of a miniature trucking farm, only they transported the produce on pack-horses. The mining camps in the area were quite receptive to the fresh vegetables and the two did a tidy little business.

The two homesteaders were fond of critters and kept an undetermined number of cats and five dogs. One of the dogs was named "Water." Four-Eyed Smith always told his guests that their dishes were as clean as "Water" could make them.

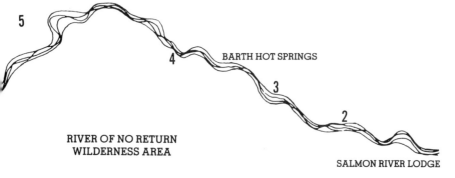

BARTH HOT SPRINGS

RIVER OF NO RETURN
WILDERNESS AREA

SALMON RIVER LODGE

LEGEND

1. The Founding of Salmon, Idaho
2. Pictographs near Stoddard Creek
3. Voices at Lantz Bar
4. Hucklebeary Pie
5. Wild Girl of the Salmon River Mountains
6. Last Pioneer of Campbell's Ferry
7. Jim Moore's Homestead
8. William Rhett's
9. The Old Painter Place
10. Buckskin Bill's
11. The Bemis Place
12. Florence

The Salmon River has an average annual flow of 7,500,000 acre feet.

All 425 miles of the Salmon River are coiled up in the timbered mountain area of the center of the state, and it has the distinction of being the longest river lying wholly within one state and of rushing through a gorge that is a fifth of a mile deeper than the Grand Canyon.

The record Chinook Salmon of Idaho weighed 42 lbs. and 8 oz. It was caught from the Salmon River by Richard Ruark in April, 1961.

"An antediluvian ark"

The First Boat Down "The River of No Return"

President Jefferson approved the Nation's first overland expedition and in 1804 the leaders, Lewis and Clark, set out to achieve history. The overland explorers turned back only once during an adventure which spanned over two years—when they faced the steep walled canyons and white waters of the Salmon River Canyon.

Thus, the Salmon remained unconquered until over ninety years later, when in October, 1886, Captain Harry Guleke piloted a flat-bottomed scow through its treacherous rapids to Riggins, Idaho.

The boat Guleke and his first mate, Dave Sandiland, built was thirty-two feet in length with twenty-eight foot sweeps with six-foot blades. It was said to resemble "an antediluvian ark sired by some prehistoric mail order packing case."

An elevated platform in the center gave the boatmen not only a sturdy foot hold but also a clearer view while navigating. The bottom of the scow was doubly lined with green lumber to give it buoyancy, lifting capacity and durability needed to withstand the shock of striking submerged rocks. A raised floor was built to keep seepage water from soaking equipment and double walls were built on each side for storage. When fully loaded, the craft weighed over four tons.

Guleke braved one rapid after another, recording the secrets of each before venturing farther into the unknown. The boat, which had taken over four days to build, was disassembled at the end of its journey and the timber put to other uses. One-way traffic on "The River of No Return" had come to stay, though boats were often smashed on hidden rocks and lives were lost.

Six years later Captain Guleke again made history on the Salmon River. The *Lewiston Tribune* reported December 20, 1902: "An odd-shaped scow landed at the wharf yesterday with three men—Captain Harry Guleke, R.E. Dwyer, and J.V. Dwyer. They made the trip from Salmon City to Lewiston via the wild Salmon—a voyage heretofore just dreamed of."

Remedies for the Stout-Hearted

Becoming ill on the river is no picnic, but should an ailment befall you, here are a few pioneer remedies which should get you back on your feet in no time.

Asthma—*Take one ounce of skunk cabbage root, one ounce of garlic, one half pound seneca snake root, half a pound of spignut, and the liver of a wolf. Boil them all in three gallons of rain water until you reduce it one half. Dose half a tablespoon three times each day one hour before eating. This has cured hundreds.*

Nervous Affections—*Take one ounce of lobelia seed, one ounce cayenne, one ounce Solomon's seal, one ounce of blue violet roots (must be blue, not yellow), one ounce green poplar, handfull of beech drops, the same quantity of Indian Pipe and put the whole in four quarts of pure Holland gin, by the fire, lightly corked for seven days, then strain and add four pounds of molasses and two quarts of rain water. This is infallible.*

Wind in the Stomach—*Take four parts dried Indian turnip, mountain ash berries, and roots of the nettle, and pulverize them and take one ounce of each of the above and put in one quart of gin and take as occasion requires.*

Pain in the Side—*Make a plaster of balsam of tamarack and wear on the side and drink tea made of bittersweet and green poplar bark.*

For Hysterics—*Take a quantity of mountain tea, white root, and unkum root, equal parts, pound them and make them into pills binding with tamarack balsam and yellow poplar; take two or three of these when the disorder is coming on. It seldom fails to arrest hysteria in progress.*

Pictographs Near Stoddard Creek

What do they mean, those stains on the sheer-faces stone near Stoddard Creek, believed to be the works of the Tukuarika (Sheepeater) Indians? It is like viewing a diary written in code and the mystery of it stirs in one the desire to know what pieces of gossip the markings reveal.

La Van Martuneau is an authority on pictographs and petroglyphs (though quite modest about the fact), and has written extensively on the subject, including his widely acclaimed book, *The Rocks Begin to Speak*.

The man, like the pictographs he studies and records, has a fascinating history. La Van, of French descent, was taken in by the Paiutes after the death of his parents. In the Paiute village just on the outskirts of Cedar City, Utah, La Van learned their language, songs and customs. He not only speaks the language of the Paiute, but also is fluent in the languages of several other tribes, including sign language. In the tradition of his adopted culture, La Van lives a nomadic lifestyle. His lodge (teepee) is often found at reservation and pow-wow celebrations across the country where he participates in competitive and ceremonial Indian war dancing.

When asked to enlighten us on the pictographs near Stoddard Creek, La Van responded, "...I'll give you what little I can on the panel you sent (photo). I don't yet know all the symbols. It also helps to be familiar with the exact area, whether it was a ford, etc., etc.

"...this one depicts a battle. The headless figures are the people killed. The two upper figures are horsemen (Indian). The one in the front is either wearing a robe or carrying a shield. Both riders have relaxed ears meaning that they were "not alert" and hence caught off guard and surprise attacked.

"Below there you see a riderless horse to indicate they dismounted during the battle. The man in front of this horse

Pictographs near Stoddard Creek

has relaxed ears also and is next to a circular device with a person inside to probably show a fortress made amidst the trees...after dismounting.

"The headless figures below are painted in a different shade of red to probably indicate the ambushers and to distinguish them from the other group. Hence two shades of red ochre were used. This shows that some of the attackers were killed since they are headless. The digits (1111111111) are probably counting devices as to the number involved (people, days?)."

The paint used on the rocks was made from mineral oxides and grease.

For those who wish to know more about pictographs and other Indian rock paintings or picture carvings, La Van's *The Rocks Begin to Speak* may be purchased directly from K.C. Publishers, P.O. Box 14883, Las Vegas, NV 89114.

Territorial Centennial Edition of the Idaho Almanac 1863-1963: *"The beautiful Salmon River drains the tremendous primative area of central Idaho. Main tributaries include the Little Salmon, the South Fork, the Middle Fork and the East Fork. The Salmon River provides excellent steelhead fishing in the spring and fall, from its confluence with the Snake River upstream for nearly 300 miles. Much of the drainage may be reached only by boat or pack outfit.*

"The Salmon River and its tributaries also have rainbow, native cutthroat, and Dolly Varden trout. There are many good mountain lakes in this drainage also. Chinook Salmon fishing is high on the activity list from late June until September along the main Salmon River."

Idaho Free Press, February 13, 1891: *"John Hadorn was up from his ranch during the week and reports that the Salmon River is so low that he forded it without the least bit of trouble. If the stage of water don't increase the salmon will make an awful dust as they climb over the bars and riffles on their way upstream in the spring."*

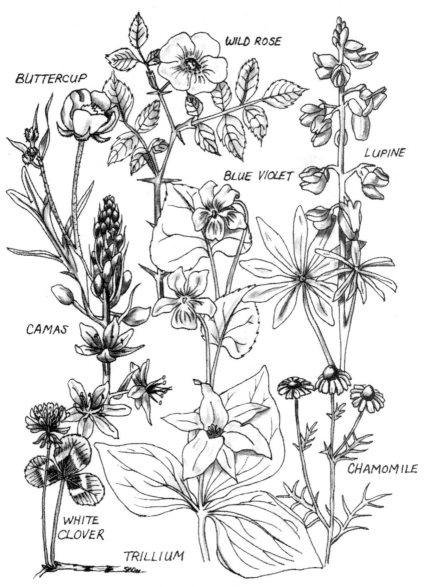

Salmon River Wild Flowers

Salmon River Wild Flowers

Along the banks of the river's channel grow numerous flowers and wild herbs. Yellow buttercups scatter across grassy spots near creek beds in the spring while trilliums show their three-petaled faces among the conifers of mountain slopes. Violets of blue, white and yellow nod on slender stems amid cool, shaded woods. Near the moist banks of fern-lined streams grow the shy, pink lady-slipper.

Camas splash across small, open meadows in late spring, sometimes growing so profusely that they resemble sky-blue ponds. The large flowered, low growing, daisy-like Wyethia, abundant among boulders of the sparsely covered slopes, fill the air with spicy fragrance in late May and early June.

The purple lupine, sego lily, Indian paint brush and larkspur dance through the sage during early summer, while pink shooting-stars color the moist areas vacated by the earlier camas. Pink wild roses, lilac-purple fireweed and snow white ever-lasting line mountain trails. Hidden amid the quiet shade of pine and cedar grows the ghostly Indian pipe.

Yarrow, goldenrod and aster-like fleabanes herald the autumn and can be found in full bloom even as the huckleberry turns red, the mountain ash wains orange and the aspen leaves flutter like hundreds of golden medallions.

Each flower and herb carries a special meaning:
Cow Slip—divine beauty
Burdock—touch me not
Camas—bounty
Chickweed—rendezvous
Daisy, wild—I will think of it
Dock—patience
Ever-lasting—never ceasing
Fireweeed—industry

Wild geranium—steadfast piety

Huckleberry—bewitching soul

Indian Pipe—illusiveness

Larkspur—lightness

Mountain ash—prudence

Wild rose—I love

Shooting-Star—romantic wishes

Violet, white—sincerity

Wythia—haughtiness

Aspen tree—lamentation

Buttercup—childishness

Camomile—energy in adversity

Clover, white—think of me

Dandelion—rustic oracle

Elder—zealousness

Fern—fascination

Fleabane—early friendship

Golden rod—precaution

Indian paintbrush—curiosity

Lady-slipper—capricious beauty

Lupine—imagination

Pine—pity

Trillium—modest beauty

Violet, blue—faithfulness

Violet, yellow—rural happiness

Yarrow—healthful

Claims

(of a few dedicated miners)

Notice is hereby given that we the undersigned claim three claims in Humburg Gulch commencing at Miller's Creek and running up to the reservoir. Oct. 29th, 1864.

J.S. Kelly & Co.

We claim the meadow situated about 12 miles almost due south from Miller's claim on Miller's Creek, for ranching purposes. Oct. 5, 1861

D. Sanberg

James Gary

I the undersigned claime three claimes for mining purposes on the head of Miller's Gulch commencing at the Large Bolder or Stump on the left hand side of the Gulch designating the line between me and the Newel D. Stoweys claime and running two Claimes up to the right hand Gulch and one up the left. August 22, 1865

Ferdinand the Frenchman

I claim one claim of 50 yds. commencing at a large dead tree and running up the gulch. Oct. 3, 1861

J.L. Lewis

Salmon River Philosophers

(The names have been changed to protect the guilty)

As seen at Isabella Bayhorse's cabin near Dead Horse Gulch.

Johnny Creek: *"Man, if my bride is sick and I tell her she looks like hell, she gets on my case. And man, if I don't notice she's sick, she gets on my case. Are all women like this, man, or is the isolation screwing her up?"*

Isabella Bayhorse: *"She must let the wind do her sighing and the clouds weep her tears. Life on the Salmon is too rich to squander on things so frivolous."*

Dynamo Dave: *"A woman rarely makes up her mind to do anything. She acts on impulse and makes up her mind afterwards."*

Harry Henpecker: *"A flirtatious woman is a rose from which every lover picks a petal and all that's left for the husband are the thorns, Johnny."*

Hilda Henpecker: *"Temptation is the worm Satan puts on his hook when fishing a promising hole. Suckers swallow the bait without much investigation. Don't they Harry? Harry? Answer me!"*

Bachelor Bob: *"It's hard to convince a crow that it doesn't know as much about music as a Canyon Wren, huh Hilda? There are a few human crows flapping around here."*

Ebenzer Fiddle: *"Johnny, there are two things in life to worry about—things you can control and things you can't. Fix the first and forget the other."*

Bachelor Bob: *"Making money and making love have a thing in common, Johnny—the more you get, the more you want. I live in the canyon without love or money. And I want for nothing."*

Dynamo Dave: *"A woman with her monthly is like a rose in a puddle of mud."*

Isabella Bayhorse: *"Throw pebbles at the world and the world will drop boulders on you, Dynamo!"*

Dynamo Dave: *"I'd rather tell the truth and run, than lie and get caught."*

Isabella Bayhorse: *"Men will promise women and children anything to keep them quiet. You blasted gimlet-heads!"*

Dynamo Dave: *"Well, Johnny, it's usually true that a man with long hair is short on something else."*

Ebenezer Fiddle: *"Don't believe all you see, Dynamo. If tombstones told the truth, the horned gentleman from the hot place would have to go out of business."*

Isabella Bayhorse: *"You might as well go out in the canyon and talk to an echo, Johnny, as to talk to a person who agrees with everything you tell them."*

Henry Henpecker: *"No one fully practices what they preach, Isabella; this is no reason not to preach. My favorite temperance lecture was delivered by Hilda, here, while under the influence of Wild Turkey."*

Hilda Henpecker: *"Harry is always telling folks he's got an iron will. That he does. One made of pig-iron."*

Harry Henpecker: *"Women are like fish. Neither would get into trouble if they kept their mouths shut."*

Ebenezer Fiddle: *"If one thinks before one speaks, one would find that 90 percent of the time there would be no occasion to say a word."*

Bachelor Bob: *"Constant craving for company and the fear of being alone is a sign of mental weakness, Johnny. Man grows in solitude. Send the bride back to Seattle."*

The Voices at Lantz Bar

It is said by some that voices are heard along a section of the Salmon known as Lantz Bar. Not eerie voices, voices of grief, or voices of sorrow and despair — but low, calm, monotone voices similar to that of a seasoned couple planning their day's routine over a cup of coffee at the kitchen table.

There was a seasoned couple who lived on the bar—Frank and Jessie Lantz. For ten years Frank had lived alone on the bar. One day he went away to Montana and when he returned he brought with him a bride. Jessie, a quiet, well-bred woman, embraced life on the Salmon. Together the couple built a two-story log home.

Under the gabled roof upstairs were two bedrooms. Most of the downstairs of the house was occupied by an L-shaped living room with a large kitchen at one corner. Here a traveler was usually treated to the fragrance of home-baked bread or the sweet, piquant scent of jam simmering on the stove. And always rich, hot coffee awaited. Or a bracing glass of Jessie's applejack.

A large structure was built over an underground basement where Jessie kept her canned goods and butter. The butter she ordered twice a year, sinking it, still wrapped in its paper, in a brine strong enough to float an egg. During autumn the floor above the cellar was full of juicy red apples, neatly sorted in bins. Most of the apples were destined to become applejack.

Frank worked for the Forest Service for twenty-seven years and panned for gold when the urge seized him. Aside handling radio messages from the fire lookouts, Jessie gardened, gathered fruits from Frank's orchard, canned, and counted her chickens at night.

Jessie died June 3, 1955, of a blood clot. She had lived at Lantz Bar for twenty years. Frank continued to live at Lantz Bar where he died October 12, 1971, after 46 years on the Salmon River. Both are buried at Corvallis, Montana, near Jessie's native home.

The home the couple had built together is gone—destroyed by fire October 14, 1971. But did Frank and Jessie really leave their paradise on Lantz Bar?

Some say the voices are merely the sound of the wind slipping down over Fawn Ridge. And some say its the water gurgling over the stones of Little Squaw Creek. Everyone is entitled to an opinion.

Lantz Bar is a good place to stretch one's legs. As you wander around the old homestead you will see the cabin built by Frank's friends—with the help of the supervisor of the Bitterroot National Forest—replacing the home lost in the 1967 fire. But look further. There on the flat—that's what's left of Frank's orchard. And over there—see the remains of Jessie's cellar?

While roaming the place, if you chance to see a woman pale of face and thin, with grayish brown hair drawn loosely back at the nape of her neck—a woman dressed in bib overalls over a gray shirt with rolled-up sleeves—ask Jessie how her applejack turned out last season. Or, while examining the orchard, you happen to spot a medium-sized gent with grey hair and scraggly beard, wearing high-topped boots, look past the old, wrinkled face and bad teeth to the youthful grin and bright impish eyes. Listen politely while he tells you of his dislike for Senator Robert Taft, then, to discreetly change the subject, ask Frank if he's still panning an average of six bucks in gold per day.

*Lewiston **Morning Tribune*** July 15, 1949. *"The 'River of No Return' lost its title with the completion of a boat trip up the Salmon. The party traveled from Riggins for 110 miles up the Middle Fork of the Salmon, which is 70 miles down river from Salmon, Idaho. Here they had to abandon the river because of low water."*

*Idaho **County Free Press*** May 25, 1902. *"Horse thieves are hiding in Salmon River country. Thomas H. Mason is dead. He settled on Mason Creek in 1868. His brother was one of the first killed in the Nez Perce War."*

The Sheepeaters

Steep granite mountains thrust their craggy profiles towards deep blue skies, oblivious of the warm-blooded beasts which scrambled along loose-shale trails criss-crossing its vertical face. The sure-footed mountain sheep made the foreboding mountains home—as did the cougar, the eagle and the Sheepeater Indians.

For over eight thousand years the Sheepeater Indians lived in peace among the remote mountains and canyons of the Salmon River country. Their environment was rugged and harsh, which led to little rivalry among other tribes since all others preferred lands where buffalo, elk and deer were abundant.

The Sheepeater people followed their ancient ways long after white man invaded the west. Because of the remoteness and inaccesibility of their home, time stood still.

The fur trade moved into Idaho, disrupting the lives of various tribes, including the Nez Perce, Shoshone and Bannocks. The Sheepeaters remained in solitude, their region remaining nearly inpenetrable. Gold was discovered in the Salmon River area and miners swarmed like flies to rotting fish. The Sheepeaters tightened their boundaries, drawing into the most primitive reaches of their region and remained, for a time, unmolested.

The Bannock and Nez Perce made Idaho history and indignant white men rounded up the renegade reds and sentenced them to generation upon generation of reservation life.

Some Bannocks took exception to this treatment and escaped to the mountains where the legendary Sheepeaters lived, still unviolated by the encroaching whites.

But life in the rugged mountains are too restricting for the once free-roaming Bannock. They had neither the skill nor the patience to become hunters of the mountain sheep.

Yet, they could never return to their homeland and the way that they had once known. Soon they were plundering the homesteads lying on the outskirts of the Sheepeaters' region. And some young Sheepeater braves, awed by the aggressive Bannock, took up the sport to show that their daring and bravery was none less than that of their war-like mentors.

Trouble had begun for the peaceable, ancient people— February, 1879, five Chinese miners were robbed and killed on Loon Creek. Two months later, Hugh Johnson and Peter Dorsey were found slain on their ranch on the South Fork of the Salmon.

Three units of troopers, with twenty Umatilla Indian scouts among them, were sent to capture or kill the Sheepeater people.

One unit found that the swollen streams were too dangerous to cross and though it was mid-July, deep snow still covered the mountains. A snowslide wiped out a string of mules carrying rations, and the troops were three days without food before they were able to down game to replenish their supplies. They found signs of Sheepeaters, but the Indians kept one mountain ahead.

Because of heavy snow pack, the second detachment, heading for the Big Creek area, had to turn back twice to seek alternate routes. After three weeks of searching, the troopers rode into a canyon ambush. Two troopers were wounded and many horses and mules fell. The detachment took cover. The Sheepeaters then set the brush in the canyon on fire. Fighting smoke and flames, the troopers retreated all the way back to base camp. The Sheepeaters followed the retreating soldiers, burning the James Rains' ranch enroute, killing one man and wounding another.

The third unit was sent after the renegades, but to no avail. While they concentrated their search near the Crooked River area, the Sheepeaters ambushed four men near the Falls of the Payette, killing three and wounding one.

On August 20, near Soldier Bar, another skirmish took place and a soldier was killed.

The deadly game of hide and seek continued until September 25, 1879. As a detachment sat before a large

Bighorn

camfire at Papoose Gulch, they heard a movement in the darkness. Then an Indian stepped into the ring of firelight. He was a chief, and in token submission, he laid down his old Henry rifle. The Sheepeaters were tired of running. Winter was to soon lock them safely in the mountains—but after winter comes spring, and with spring more detachments. The people knew that eventually the end of the trail would come.

The Sheepeaters, their numbers less than 200, were placed in confinement on the reservation located on the flats of Fort Hall.

A small band of Sheepeaters, under Chief Eagle Eye, remained illusive—remained free—amid the Salmon River Mountains until the 1900s.

Hucklebeary Pie

You could get to "Andy the Russian's" cabin by following a trail up the south bank of the Salmon River. Andy Strauss built his log home on the edge of a large clearing and planted the customary garden with some fruit trees. He lived a frugal life, growing great quanities of flowers, and was also known to perform the daily routine in his preferred attire, "naked." There was a bell hung at the top of the trail for visitors to ring—and give Andy a chance to pull on a pair of shorts.

A homesteader from down-river accepted a bear steak dinner invitation from Andy one evening. For dessert he was served huckleberry pie. After eating it he asked the Russian where he had found the huckleberries. "Oh, I found them in the bear's stomach," replied Andy.

"Hucklebeary Pie"

Wild Girl of the Salmon River Mountains

The year of 1877 was not a good year for the miners, ranchers and homesteaders along the Salmon River. The Nez Perce Indians were on the warpath. Many of the settlers were able to make their way to Freedom, a settlement on Slate Creek where a stockade was being built to enclose the houses and buildings.

Other settlers, widely scattered up and down the river with homesteads tucked away in ravines, chose to stay and protect their homes from plunder. Here women and children huddled together while the men took their posts by the windows. Many spent the entire length of the siege thus, with nary a savage seen.

Others watched groups of sixteen to twenty braves descend on their humble homesteads, war cries echoing through the canyons and up the ravines. Rifle shots rang out. Homesteaders and Indians fell. Glass shattered— doorways splintered, acrid wood smoke snaked through the air as the sounds of crackling, snapping flames and war whoops assaulted the ear. Some of the women and children were slaughtered, some were left huddling in fear and some were carried away on the sweaty backs of spotted rumped war ponies. There braves of the scattered bands each dealt with the situations as they saw fit—or according to whim.

The Holbrooks, cattle ranchers along the Salmon, fought valiantly for their home. But soon the ranch hands lay dead at their posts. Mr. Holbrook, too, fell and was left for dead. His wife and three-year-old daughter were carried away to the hills.

Smoke from the burning buildings drew aide from neighboring ranchers. They found Mr. Holbrook stunned from a head wound and no sign of his daughter or wife. Several days later his wife was found wandering the hills.

She had been tortured before her release. Her little three-year-old daughter was thought to be dead.

Some time later the Holbrooks moved to Colorado to try to heal their emotional wounds and begin anew. Mrs. Holbrook, in spite of her husband's tender administrations, never recovered from the injuries and shock.

Nine years later a hunter passed through a dense forest in the depth of the Salmon River Mountains far from the dwellings of man, and discovered a beautiful, untrodden grassy valley bordering what is now known as Moose Lake. At the far end of the valley, tapering to the lake, were columns of moss covered granite with yawning black caverns. As the hunter stood in awe at the panorama spread before him, he saw a young, fair-haired maiden spring from the water and disappear into one of the caverns.

The hunter returned to his camp and three comrades with the story of the girl. The three hunters sat around the campfire that night jeering at his tale, but come morning, they ventured to the meadow.

There she stood at the foot of the cliff at the water's edge, draped in the skins of the wild beasts. The men had difficulty believing what they saw, and as they pondered, the girl disappeared.

The four returned to the settlements along the Salmon where their story was told and retold. A newspaper correspondent got wind of the tale and rounded up a few daring cowboys to accompany him to the rumored place in search of the legendary girl.

At length they found the valley, the lake, and the columns of granite with their numerous caverns. But not a sign of the girl. After searching in vain they prepared to leave. Then there! Were those not unevenly worn stone steps? And did they not appear to be leading to the doorway of a primitive, subterranean home?

The men approached the opening and hallooed. There was a stir within, then a form appeared, barring the entrance to the cavern. It was an ancient, feeble Indian with tangled strings of grey hair. He viewed the men with watery red eyes, the withered form of a palsied arm outstretched as if to hold the strangers at bay.

So this is the wild girl—the maiden draped in the skins of

wild beasts—the newspaper correspondent chuckled to himself. Yet, something in the old Indian's eyes alerted the reporter. He pushed the ancient man aside and entered a winding tunnel which led to a great cavern with angular recesses and uneven ceilings and walls. Columns of stone divided the vast interior into compartments. His torch light fell on a girl, of about twelve years of age, cowering on a pallet of animal hides. Her fear of the intruders appeared to be so great that they backed away and exited the cave.

One of the cowpokes spoke Nez Perce and attempted to communicate with the old Indian. The ancient, feeble warrior had no tongue and could only communicate with sign language. It became understood that the old man, a member of the Nez Perce, was the father of Eagle Eye and the grandfather of Chuck. Many, many years back he had displeased his tribe and was condemned to have his tongue cut out and banished. He came to live in the broody caves of Moose Lake.

Wild Girl of the Salmon River Mountains

On occasion, the old man left the remote region to travel to the settlements along the Salmon River where he traded furs for powder and lead. One such journey led to the discovery of the small captured child. He rescued her and became her provider and protector. Fish, game, roots and berries were their food; the skins of wild animals, their clothing.

The correspondent and cowboys left the peaceful, high mountain valley. A story was written about the old palsied Indian and the young wild white girl. Newspapers throughout the west published the unusual account.

Several weeks later, in Colorado, Mr. Holbrook picked up a newspaper and chanced across the account. He hastened to the Salmon River Country, convinced that the child was his lost daughter. A party was organized, including two of the cowpokes who had made the previous trip.

The party arrived at the meadow and made their way to the caverns. The old Indian was guarding the entrance. Mr. Holbrook cast the frail man aside and rushed into the cave. Upon seeing the girl, he called out her name and embraced her. She flew at him, clawing and fighting. Her strength was such that he was flung against the walls of the cave as the girl fled to her protector.

One of the cowhands signed to the old man telling, to the best of his ability, of the situation—of Mr. Holbrook's need for his daughter and of the young girl's need to be reared among her own people. The old man understood, and after great deliberation, decided that it would be best for the child to be returned to her people. In sign language he related the situation to his young charge. She refused to go of her own accord, but with much persuasion, and some force, Mr. Holbrook and his party managed to get the girl to the home of a friend living along the Salmon. The old Indian accompanied the party and aided in the work of taming the girl before she was to be separated from the only person who could communicate with her.

In the end, the girl went with her father to Colorado. The old Indian returned to the cave—a suddenly empty, solitary, joyless place—where he lived out his remaining days.

The Last Pioneer of Campbell's Ferry

Frances Wisner called herself a 'throwback' to a more peaceful era, a 19th century soul displaced in the 20th century. As a young woman she worked as a telephone operator in Beeville, Texas. At night the operators would talk to one another to keep awake. For Frances the favorite topic was finding a place where the clock stopped, where it didn't make any difference what day it was. "I said I would find it some day and never leave. I did and I didn't," she said.

Her wilderness home on the Salmon River lived up to that image. The rustic log cabin borders the river on one side and a lush green meadow on the other. An ample garden with a creek for irrigation supplied most of her food. Plus a well-established apple orchard that also attracted bears, moose, elk and deer. Wisner recalled shooting at least 8 bears in her front yard.

Since Frances showed up at Campbell's Ferry in 1941, "with just a toothbrush," she firmly planted her roots for good. At the time Joe Zaunmiller owned and operated the ferry, as well as being a packer and guide. He was soon to become Frances' first husband. After his death Wisner married a second time and was widowed again in 1974. Her only resident companion after that was Gretchin, a German shepherd.

The activity around Campbell's Ferry actually decreased after the Forest Service installed a bridge to replace the ferry in 1956. The gold boom had ended and traffic was limited to backpackers and boaters in the summer months. Solitude was what Frances had come for and she never tired of it. Her contact with the outside was through a weekly mail and supply flight, perhaps the last airplane post office route in the United States.

Frances Wisner

The local town of Grangeville also kept in touch with Frances via a weekly column she wrote for the paper since 1945. "You wonder what there would be to write about being back here all by myself? Plenty!" she said, "Plenty!" Once Weisner took on the hunters and got a bill passed that made it illegal to shoot wild animals from aircraft. "It was one helluva battle. I was really ostracized, if you can imagine anybody living in the middle of nowhere being ostracized. But I didn't give a damn."

Her lifestyle was not unlike the pioneers from 100 years earlier. Francis Zaunmiller Wisner died in 1986 at 72 years of age, with her wish fulfilled. As she said, "Just look at the beauty of the river, the mountains. It's all mine. Can you blame me for never leaving?"

Free Press *November 29, 1981: "The iron bridge across the Salmon River (at French Creek) cannot be built this year. In the first place, the same company had a contract to build a bridge across the Spokane River, near Spokane. By some oversight, the Spokane bridge was shipped to Weiser and the Salmon River bridge was shipped to Spokane. The Spokane bridge is 50 feet shorter than the Salmon River bridge. When the Salmon bridge was shipped to Weiser, no one would undertake to haul it to French Creek for fear of being snowed in, consequently the bridge is still at Weiser."*

The Salmon River rises amid rugged peaks of the Sawtooth Range, over 10,000 feet high and flows through valleys and canyons to its confluence with the Snake River near where Oregon, Washington and Idaho meet. In 390 miles it falls more than a vertical mile.

The Salmon River Canyon is one of the deepest and most rugged in North America. From rim to river its depth in several places exceeds 6,000 feet—more than that of the equally wide Grand Canyon.

Dwarfs of the Salmon River Caves

Dwarfs of the Salmon River Caves

The Shoshoni and Bannock men used to tell of a race of cannibalistic dwarfs who lived in the caves of the Salmon River Country. These 2-feet tall people with long tails could carry elk, deer and mountain sheep on their backs. The women dressed in animal skins but the men wore no clothing at all, even in winter.

The Shoshoni and Bannock rarely ventured into the area of these dwarfs, for the women would not have dared to get out of the sight of their babies or children. The little devils would seize any baby left unguarded and gobble it up. Then the dwarf would cry the eaten baby's cry to draw its mother near. The nasty dwarfs would then attack the mother and begin devouring her. The desperate woman's screams would scare the evil little varmits away—but she would always die of her vicious wounds.

The dwarfs could fool children by winding their tails around their bodies to conceal their true identities, then coax the children into play. Soon they would run off with the gullible children astride their tails. And the children would never be heard from again.

The dwarfs never ate Indian men. In fact, the Shoshone and Bannock men who ventured into the Salmon River area were frequently fed and entertained in the caves of these miniature monsters.

It all sounds pretty fishy to me. Especially since comely Sheepeater women lived in the high reaches of the Salmon River country.

Territorial Centennial Edition of the Salmon Almanac
1863-1963 *"The best time to view the Salmon River Canyon*
is in the late afternoon or at sunset when the soft golden
rays of light blend with the myriad-colored canyon walls to
produce a scene of breathtaking beauty. Although some
portions of the canyon are extremely narrow and impassa-
ble and in places it reaches a depth of over a mile, making
it in those places the second deepest canyon in the United
States (second only to Hell's Canyon), the Salmon River
Canyon is not noted, for the most part, for sheer walls and
towering heights. Rather it is remembered for its variety of
monuments, the bluffs and slides, the picturesque castles
and towers, the gentle, wood-carpeted slopes, the solitary
crags—and the exquisite coloring of the stones.

Salmon River Canyon

Salmon River Outfitter's Gourmet Menu

Gourmet Magazine chose the Salmon River Outfitter's trip down the main Salmon for a feature story which appeared in their July, 1988 issue. Recipes from this white water trip have also appeared in *Sunset* and *Bon Appetit.* Here is a generous sampling of their renown cuisine, beginning with breakfasts which herald each exciting morning along "The River of No Return."

Gruyere Souffle *(serves 10)*

10 eggs
½ cup butter
2 cups milk
1 lb. gruyere cheese, grated
1 bunch green onions, chopped
⅔ cup unbleached flour
1 tsp. baking soda
½ tsp. baking powder
¼ tsp. cream of tartar
½ tsp. freshly ground pepper

Separate eggs. Add cream of tartar to egg whites and set aside. Saute green onions in butter. Beat together egg yolks and milk. Slowly beat in flour. Pour into large skillet and heat over medium flame until mixture simmers and thickens. Add cheese and stir until melted. Remove from heat.

Whisk whites until soft peaks form. Stir one-third of the beaten whites into cooled sauce. Quickly fold in baking powder and soda, then fold sauce into remaining whites. Spoon into a greased 12-inch Dutch oven and bake in hot coals for approximately 25 minutes.

"Imagine—duck with currant sauce and cheese souffle right on the shores of a wild river in Idaho! We were eating as if we were in a fine restaurant, but were miles from civilization."

Sunset Magazine

Banana Walnut Buttermilk Pancakes with Yogurt Topping *(serves 20 to 25)*

> *4 cups whole wheat flour*
> *4 cups unbleached flour*
> *2½ tsp. baking powder*
> *2½ tps. baking soda*
> *1½ cups packed brown sugar*
> *2 cups roasted broken walnuts*
> *9 medium-sized eggs, separated*
> *¾ cup safflower oil*
> *6 large, ripe bananas, peeled and mashed*
> *3 (approximately) cups buttermilk*

Sift together dry ingredients. Separate egg whites. Beat whites until stiff peaks form. Set aside.

Beat together egg yolks, oil and milk. Stir in bananas, then blend into dry ingredients. Do not stir out all lumps. Adjust milk for thicker or thinner batter, depending on taste. Fold in egg whites.

Yogurt Topping:

> *2 quarts vanilla flavored yogurt*
> *1 cup chopped, roasted walnuts*
> *2 cups chopped dates*
> *1½ cups sweetened coconut*

Mix together topping ingredients. Chill.

On lightly greased griddle, bake pancakes until air bubbles on surface break, then turn and bake on other side.

Asparagus and Cheese Egg Puff *(serves 25 to 30)*

18 eggs
1 lb. Cheddar cheese, grated
2 lb. bulk sausage
1 bunch green onions, chopped
1½ lbs. fresh asparagus
1 cup heavy cream
½ tsp. white pepper
3 cups milk
1 cup flour
2 tsp. baking soda
1 tsp. baking powder

Brown sausage in skillet and drain fat. Divide between two Dutch ovens. In steamer basket, steam fresh trimmed asparagus until soft; puree two-thirds of the asparagus and stir in cream and white pepper. Combine with beaten eggs and chopped green onions. Mix well. Sift together flour, baking soda and baking powder. Stir into egg mixture. Spoon over sausage in Dutch oven. Sprinkle a little extra cheese and a few chopped onion tops on surface. Arrange the remaining asparagus spears in a circle on top.

Bake in hot coals until puff has set and it has turned golden brown on top (usually 25 to 35 minutes).

"While the main attraction remains the river and its pristine environment, the appeal of poached salmon washed down with good wine cannot be under-estimated. Armed with four Dutch ovens and a propane stove, the crew turns out fresh bread, blueberry coffeecakes, and gruyere souffles."

The New York Times

French Toast with Yogurt Topping

(serves 25 to 30)

12 eggs
1 cup milk
1 cup heavy cream
1 Tbsp. almond extract
4 loaves raisin bread

Topping:

1 quart vanilla flavored yogurt
1 cup chopped roasted walnuts
½ cup chopped dates
½ cup shredded sweetened coconut

Beat together eggs, milk and extract. Dip bread in mixture and brown on griddle which has been lightly oiled.

Combine topping ingredients and serve with French Toast.

The Salmon River Outfitters also have pure maple syrup for those who want an alternative to the topping.

All breakfasts served on the Salmon River Outfitter's trips are accompanied by fresh fruit, juice, milk and pots of freshly ground coffee.

Somewhere along a fine stretch of sandy beach a noon camp is set for a brief rest and lunch. As rafters stretch their legs and explore the trails or seek out wildflowers growing within the canyon, the guides set about preparing a gourmet lunch. The first such meal along the river is usually a lavish spread of cold cuts, fancy mustards and pickles.

Blueberry Coffee Cake

3 cups whole wheat flour
3 cups unbleached flour
¼ cup baking soda
3 Tbsp. baking powder
3 cups brown sugar
2 cups butter
8 eggs
3 cups milk
4 cups commercial sour cream
6 cups fresh blueberries or huckleberries (or 2 1-lb. pkgs. frozen blueberries)

Melt butter. Add eggs and sour cream. Blend in dry ingredients along with enough milk to make a medium batter. Fold in berries. Pour into two well-oiled 12-inch Dutch ovens.

Topping:

1 cup brown sugar
1 cup butter
2 cups toasted broken walnuts

With fingertips, work butter into brown sugar and nuts. Sprinkle over batter in Dutch oven. Cover with tight-fitting lid, place in hot coals and bake for 30 to 40 minutes.

Mom's Potato Salad

24 medium-sized red potatoes, unpeeled
12 medium-sized hard-cooked eggs, peeled
2 large Walla Walla sweet onions, peeled and diced
1½ bunches celery, chopped (leaves included)
1 large jar sweet gerkins, chopped

Halve eggs and remove yolks. Mash yolks in separate bowl and set aside. Chop egg whites and set aside.

Scrub potatoes, cube and place in steamer basket. Steam with a small amount of water until cooked but still firm. Set aside to cool. When cooled, gently toss with egg whites, onion, celery and gerkins. Place in colander lined with paper towels, cover with additional paper towels and chill.

Dressing:

3½ cups mayonnaise
½ cup prepared mustard
2 Tbsp. cider vinegar
1 tsp. seasoned salt
2 tsp. celery seed
½ tsp. dried rosemary
½ tsp. dried oregano
½ dried thyme
½ tsp. ground sage
1 tsp. Hungarian paprika
1 tsp. coarse pepper
1 large clove garlic, pressed
2 tsp. granulated sugar
½ cup finely chopped fresh parsley

Combine dressing ingredients and mix well. Stir 1½ cups dressing into potato mixture. Pack potato mixture into a one-gallon zip-locked bag and keep cold until ready to serve. Place remaining dressing in a zip-locked bag to be stirred into potato salad just prior to serving.

Tuna Stuffed Tomatoes

1 tomato per person
5 cans tuna
1 bunch celery, chopped
1 lb. Cheddar cheese, grated
1½ cups roasted cashews
1 red onion, chopped and soaked in cold water 30 minutes, then drained
Mayonnaise, as needed
Mustard
1 head Iceberg lettuce

Cut tomatoes into star and spread. Stuff with mixture. Sprinkle with paprika and dried parsley. Serve on lettuce leaves and garnish with carrot sticks, apple and orange wedges.

Tuna Stuffed Tomatoes

Chicken Salad in Crouisants *(serves 30)*

30 crouisants, split lengthwise
12 chicken breasts
4 cups sliced celery
3 cups seedless grapes
6 Golden Delicious apples, peeled, cored and diced
1½ cups golden raisins
1½ cups roasted walnut pieces
3 medium-sized avocados
1 lemon
2 cups mayonnaise
1 tsp. vegetable salt
½ tsp. coarsely ground pepper

Place breasts in kettle with water to cover and simmer until flesh has lost all its pink. Skin breasts, remove meat from bones and shred. Place shredded meat in large bowl and add celery, grapes, apples, raisins, and walnuts. Peel and pit avocados, then cut into pieces. Squeeze juice of lemon over avocado pieces, then add to ingredients in bowl. Mix together mayonnaise and seasonings; then fold into chicken salad. Fill split crouisants with salad mixture and serve at once.

Chicken Salad in Crouisants

"Steven Shephard's outdoor meals—all made from fresh ingredients—have been featured in gourmet magazines."
Harper's Bazaar

Green Salad

> *4 heads red leaf lettuce*
> *1 box cherry tomatoes*
> *2 cucumbers, peeled, scored and sliced*
> *1 red onion, cut into thin crescents and soaked in cold*
> *   water for 30 minutes*
> *3 jars marinated artichoke hearts*

Toss ingredients in chilled bowl. Serve with dressing made by combining 1 pkg. ranch dressing mix, mayonnaise, buttermilk and oil from marinated artichokes.

Cheese Ball

> *24 oz. cream cheese*
> *1 lb. grated Cheddar cheese*
> *Mayonnaise*
> *½ cup roasted, slivered almonds*
> *8 oz. chopped dates*
> *1 pita bread per person*

Blend cream cheese and dates with most of the Cheddar and almonds. Mix in enough mayonnaise to bind. Coat outside with remaining grated Cheddar and almonds. Mold and place on chilled platter.

> *1 head Iceberg lettuce, shredded*

Guests line up to fill their pitas with lettuce and a generous portion of the cheese ball. Then they move on down the line for a heaping portion of:

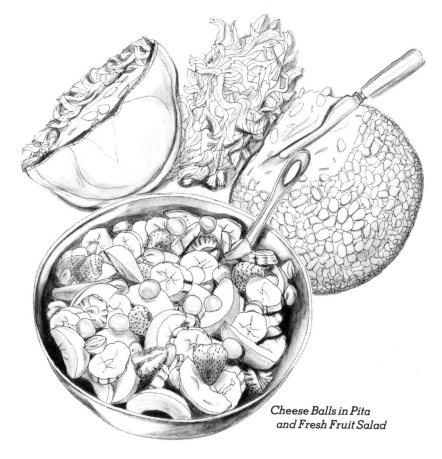

*Cheese Balls in Pita
and Fresh Fruit Salad*

Fresh Fruit Salad

*½ watermellon, seeded and cubed
6 bananas, peeled and sliced
6 peaches/nectarines, pitted and sliced
1 cantaloupe
1 honeydew
6 plums, pitted and sliced
4 apples, cored and cubed
½ lb. seedless red and green grapes*

Combine fruits and fill watermelon half shell. Toss salad with the juice of one lemon and 1 to 2 tablespoonfuls of powdered sugar.

The last meal on the river is lunch the fifth day. A platter of sliced turkey graces a makeshift table. Cranberry jelly and sauce, mustards, cheeses, onions and lettuce are loaded on one end and a variety of breads are piled on the other. As guests prepare sandwiches from the selection, canyon wrens warble among the crannies of the cliffs.

Evenings are always special treasures along the Salmon. Camp is made early so that rafters have plenty of time to set up their tents, explore, fish, take photographs or just relax with a cold glass of wine and some tasty appetizers.

Gouda-Clam Dip

3 cans minced clams
2 small Gouda cheeses
½ cup dry vermouth
1½ pints sour cream
1 cup minced onion

Cube cheese and place in food processor. Add juice from 2 cans clams and the vermouth. Process until smooth and creamy. Turn into a bowl and stir in sour cream and drained clams. Add onion and mix well.

Artichoke Dip for Raw Vegetables

4 14-oz. cans artichoke hearts
2 jars marinated artichoke hearts, drained
½ cup Parmesan cheese
½ cup grated gruyere cheese
2 cloves garlic, cut into pieces
2 cups mayonnaise

In food processor, finely chop marinated artichoke hearts. Set aside. Drain the 4 cans of artichoke hearts and place them in food processor along with mayonnaise, garlic and cheese. Process until smooth. Turn out into a bowl and stir in chopped marinated hearts. Serve with assorted vegetable dippers.

Gouda-Clam Dip

Antipasto

> 1 salami, sliced
> 1 jar red cherry peppers
> ½ lb. Cheddar cheese, cut into cubes
> ½ lb. Monterey jack, cut into cubes
> 1 can black olives, well-drained
> 1 jar kosher-style dill pickles
> 1 bunch green onions, trimmed
> 1 bunch radishes, trimmed
> Assorted crackers

Arrange ingredients attractively on platter.

This is a popular dip at cocktail parties around the country, and has lost no favor among the floaters of the river.

Spinach Dip

3 large pkgs. spinach, drained and squeezed dry
3 pkgs. Knorr Leek soup mix
3 cans water chestnuts, chopped
3 bunches green onions, chopped
3 cups mayonnaise
1½ 16-oz. containers of sour cream

Combine ingredients and serve with vegetable dippers and/or crackers.

"All meals are prepared by the trip leader, Steven Shephard, and the camp fare is likely to range from fresh salmon with wild rice to chicken enchiladas, pastas, banana nut pancakes and, by reputation, wonderful desserts."

Food and Wine Magazine

Just as the light begins to wain, dinner is dished up. Campers relax around a blazing campfire while enjoying their expertly prepared meals.

Fresh Trout

Fresh Salmon *(for thirty)*

2 6-7 lb. fresh, whole salmon

Marinade:
⅔ cup vermouth
½ cup safflower oil
⅔ cup freshly squeezed lime juice
¼ cup freshly minced parsley
¼ cup freshly minced celery leaves
3 cloves garlic, pressed
1 tsp. grated lime rind
2 tsp. finely chopped shallot
½ tsp. salt

Combine marinade ingredients and pour into jar. Keep chilled until ready to use.

Place salmon on large cast iron griddle and pour marinade over fish. Cook over medium heat until fish flakes easily, turning once with large spatulas. Garnish with fresh parsley and thin slices of lemon.

Shrimp and Pasta all Pizzaiola

Shrimp and Pasta alla Pizzaiola

5 lbs. medium-size shrimp
1 Tbsp. pickling spice
1 lb. fresh mushrooms, sliced
Olive oil
1 bunch fresh basil
1 bunch fresh parsley
2 cloves garlic, minced
Juice of 2 lemons
Pizzaiola Sauce (recipe follows)
4 cups cherry tomatoes
½ cup capers
10 oz. Feta cheese
1½ cups Romano cheese, grated
Fresh pasta for 30

Bring 2½ quarts water to boiling over high heat. Add pickling spices and shrimp. Boil for 4½ to 5 minutes, or until shrimp turns pink and curls. Cool under cold running water. Peel and devein.

Heat a small amount of olive oil in large cast iron skillet. Add sliced mushrooms and garlic. Saute 5 minutes. Tear basil and parsley into pieces and add to mushrooms along with shrimp and juice of two lemons. Cook 5 minutes. Add Pizzaiola Sauce and heat through.

In large kettle, bring 5 quarts of water to boiling. Add pasta and cook al dente. Rinse in cold running water. Toss with shrimp/sauce mixture, Feta, capers and cherry tomatoes. Sprinkle with Romano and serve at once.

Pizzaiola Sauce:

In large kettle heat 1 cup olive oil until a light haze forms over it. Remove pan from heat and add ⅓ cup finely chopped garlic and 2 seeded, finely chopped green peppers. Turn in oil for about 30 seconds. Peel, seed and coarsely chop 12 vine-ripened tomatoes and add to oil along with 1 Tbsp. fresh oregano leaves, 1 tsp. salt and 1 tsp. coarsely ground pepper. Return skillet to moderate heat and cook until most of the liquid from tomatoes has boiled away. Stir in 1 Tbsp. granulated sugar and 1 cup dry red wine.

Marinated Vegetable Salad

2 jars pimento strips, drained
3 jars marinated artichoke hearts
3 jars marinated mushrooms
1 head cauliflower, broken into flowerettes
1 lb. Chinese snow peas
½ lb. baby carrots, scraped
1 head broccoli, broken into flowerettes
1 bunch fresh cilantro, washed and torn
2 red onions, cut into rings and separated
Italian Dressing (recipe follows)

In vegetable steamer, steam cauliflower, snow peas, carrots and broccoli until tender-crisp. While still hot, pour over Italian Dressing. Add artichoke hearts, pimento, cilantro and red onions. Marinate overnight.

Italian Dressing

Marinade from artichoke hearts
Marinade from mushrooms
1 cup olive oil
½ cup white wine vinegar
½ cup freshly squeezed lemon juice
½ cup grated onion
3 Tbsp. grated Parmesan cheese
4 cloves garlic, crushed
2 Tbsp. fresh minced basil
1 tsp. dried oregano
1 tsp. dry mustard
2 tsp. salt
1 tsp. honey
¼ tsp. dried crushed red pepper

Combine dressing ingredients and mix well. Pour over steamed vegetables while vegetables are still hot.

Dutch Oven Beer Bread

6 cups whole wheat flour
6 cups unbleached flour
2 tsp. baking soda
2 tsp. baking powder
1½ cups brown sugar
2-3 cans warm beer
½ cup butter, melted

Sift together flours, baking powder and baking soda. Gently spoon into a one-gallon zip-lock bag. Spoon brown sugar into a zip-lock sandwich bag and place sealed bag in gallon bag with flour and zip closed.

At baking time, pour flour and brown sugar into a large bowl, add warm beer and stir until most of the lumps have disappeared. Do not over mix. Pour batter into a 12-inch, well-oiled Dutch oven, cover with heavy lid and place in hot coals. Bake 25 minutes. Pour melted butter over top of loaf, return to coals and continue baking until done (usually 10 minutes longer, but baking time varies with the temperature and amount of coals).

Dutch Oven Beer Bread

"A river rafting trip with the Salmon River Outfitters in Idaho proved to be more than just a sporting adventure—it was a culinary one as well.   Their Chicken Enchiladas really hit the spot after a hard day of rafting."

Irv Kodimer—Bon Appetit Magazine

Chicken Enchiladas *(serves 10)*

> 10 chicken breasts, skinned and boned
> 1 12-oz. bottle Mexican beer
> Garlic to taste
> 2 tsp. cayenne

Sauce:

> 16 oz. sour cream
> ½ cup butter
> ½ lb. fresh mushrooms, finely chopped
> ⅓ cup chicken bouillon granules
> ½ cup flour
> 4½ cups canned milk
> ½ tsp. salt
> 3 bunches green onions, chopped
> 3 cans black olives, diced
> 3 cans diced chili peppers
> 1 lb. medium Cheddar cheese, grated
> 1 lb. Monterey jack cheese, cubed
> 1 Tbsp. cumin seed, crushed
> 24 corn tortillas
> 1 dozen large flour tortillas
> 4 cups grated sharp Cheddar cheese

Cut chicken breasts into chunks and simmer in beer, in which garlic and cayenne has been added, for 15 to 20 minutes. Meanwhile make sauce.

To make sauce, melt butter in heavy skillet. Sauté mushrooms in butter in flour and cook, stirring until mixture begins to thicken. Slowly stir in milk. Add salt and onions, then stir in sour cream.

Remove chicken from marinade. Stir chicken into the sauce and add enough of the marinade to thin sauce slightly. To chicken/sauce mixture, add diced black olives, diced chili peppers, cheese and cumin. Mix well.

Grease two 12-inch Dutch ovens. Layer 2 flour and corn tortillas in each oven. Spoon some of the chicken mixture over tortillas. Repeat layers. Sprinkle top layer of each with 2 cups grated sharp Cheddar cheese, cover with lid and bake in hot coals for 45 minutes to 1 hour.

Another form of these enchiladas are served by the Salmon River Outfitters, made with a spicy tomato sauce in place of the white sauce with mushrooms. The sauce is mixed with the simmered chicken breasts and spooned over tortilla layers, then dotted with spoonfuls of sour cream. The tomato sauce version is as follows:

10 cups tomato puree
4 cups water
2 cups finely chopped onion
6 cloves garlic
10 bouillon cubes
1 Tbsp. chili powder
2 finely chopped fresh jalapeno peppers
1 tsp. cumin seed, crushed
1 bunch chopped fresh cilantro

Combine and simmer until slightly thickened. Then combine simmered chicken with sauce. Stir in:

3 bunches green onions, chopped
3 cans black olives, sliced
12 peeled and roasted ancho chilies, chopped
1½ lb. Cheddar cheese, grated
1 lb. Monterey Jack cheese, grated
1 Tbsp. ground cumin

If the gourmet river guests want additional spiciness, a side of homemade salsa is offered:

Homemade Salsa

> *5 lbs. vine-ripened tomatoes, washed and stem ends removed*
> *1½ cups finely chopped Walla Walla sweet onion*
> *2 fresh jalapeno, seeded and chopped*
> *5 cloves garlic, minced*
> *½ cup minced fresh cilantro*
> *¼ tsp. cayenne pepper*
> *2 tsp. red wine vinegar*
> *1 Tbsp. honey*
> *1 Tbsp. chili powder*
> *Juice of 2 limes*
> *1 tsp. grated lime peel*

Chop tomatoes and drain off about ⅓ of the juice. Add remaining ingredients and mix well. This salsa keeps refrigerated for up to 7 days.

Parsley Potatoes

> *20 red potatoes*
> *1 bunch parsley, minced*
> *1½ cups butter*
> *Salt and pepper to taste*

Boil potatoes; drain well. Add butter, and as it melts, stir to break potatoes into chunks. Stir in parsley.

Cabbage Salad

> *1 large head green cabbage, shredded*
> *1 large head purple cabbage, shredded*
> *1 red onion, cut into rings*
> *4 lbs. fresh cooked salad shrimp*
> *1 packet Ranch herb dressing mix*
> *3 avocados, peeled, seeded and mashed*

In large bowl toss together cabbages, onion and shrimp. Mix together dressing mix, reserved juice from shrimp and avacados. Stir into cabbage mixture.

Dessert is not to be missed on the Salmon River. A treat awaits the sweet-tooth of each camper at the end of the evening's meal.

Peach Pandowdy

20 medium-sized fresh ripe peaches
2 cups granulated sugar mixed with 2½ Tbsp. corn-
    starch

Topping:

1½ cups rolled rye flakes
1½ cups rolled oats
1½ cups brown sugar
½ cup whole wheat flour
1 cup softened butter
1 tsp. cinnamon
½ tsp. mace
1½ cups broken, toasted pecans

Combine topping ingredients in a large bowl. With fingertips, work butter and brown sugar into dry ingredients. Pour mixture into a large zip-lock bag and keep cool until used.

Peel and pit peaches. Slice into a 12-inch Dutch oven, sprinkle with sugar/cornstarch mixture, then top with topping mixture. Cover and place in hot coals. Bake for 40 to 45 minutes.

Chocolate-Carmel-Fruit Dessert

2 pkg. semi-sweet chocolate chips
6 oz. carmel sauce
12 cups frozen cherries or berries
8 bananas
1 cup Grand Marnier Liqueur
2 cups toasted sliced almonds

Melt chocolate and carmel over low heat. Add liqueur after heat is turned off. Pour over cold berries and banana slices. Top with toasted almonds and serve with amarettini cookies.

Lemon Yogurt Parfait

4 pkgs. lemon cookies
20 lemon drops
3 large containers whipped topping or
    1½ pints cream
1 quart lemon flavored yogurt
3 lemons, sliced into rings

In food processor, whirl cookies and lemon drops until all has been reduced to crumbs. Seal in zip-lock bag until needed. Fold together whipped cream and lemon yogurt. In clear plastic cups alternate layers of the cream mixture and crushed cookies. Garnish with lemon twists.

Down Home Brownies with Pecans

2 cups Ghirardelli cocoa
3 cups sugar
½ cup instant coffee crystals
2½ cups sifted cake flour
1½ tsp. baking powder
2 cups roasted pecan halves

Mix ingredients and pour into a one-gallon zip-lock bag. At time of preparation, pour dry ingredients into a large bowl and add:

1½ cups butter, melted
6 eggs beaten
3 tsp. vanilla extract
2 12-oz. pkgs. chocolate chips

Mix well before stirring into dry ingredients. Turn into a well-oiled 12-inch Dutch oven, cover with tight-fitting lid and place on hot coals. Place hot coals on top of oven for even baking. Bake 30 to 40 minutes.

French Vanilla Ice Cream

4 cups milk
6 egg yolks, slightly beaten
1 cup sugar
Dash salt
2 cups heavy cream
1½ Tbsp. vanilla extract

Mix sugar, salt and egg yolks. Pour milk over mixture. Cook in double boiler until mixture coats spoon. Cool, strain and add cream and vanilla. Freeze in hand-cranked ice cream freezer, using plenty of ice and rock salt.

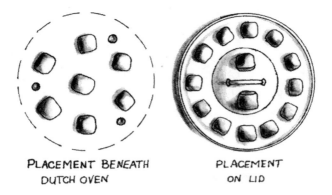

PLACEMENT BENEATH   PLACEMENT
DUTCH OVEN   ON LID

Dutch Oven Instructions

The recipes compiled in this book have been prepared outdoors in the pouring rain as well as in the test kitchens of *Bon Appetit* and *Gourmet* magazines. Those that require baking can be smoothly produced at home in a glass pyrex pan, or along side a campfire in a metal Dutch oven. With practice, both should become equally successful.

The Dutch oven (D.O.) best suited to fireside baking is a round cast iron or aluminum pot. Common sizes vary from 8 to 16 inches in diameter, and 4 to 6 inches deep. The lid should be flat and have a vertical lip around the outside edge to retain coals. Many models have 3 legs which are convenient for spacing the bottom from hot coals. It should also have a balanced bail for lifting and carrying.

Cast Iron

This is the heavier model with certain advantages when weight is not a factor. It holds heat better than aluminum and the lid can be preheated directly over the campfire flames.

A new cast iron D.O. needs to be seasoned with cooking oil. Rub the inside with a liberal coating and heat it at home in the oven (300 degrees F.) or over the stove-top (low heat). Remove the D.O. when it starts to smoke and wipe off excess oil with paper towels. After using and washing, re-oil lightly to keep seasoned and prevent rusting.

Aluminum

This style is one-third the weight of an equal size cast iron model. It needs no seasoning and is rust-proof. Because of its light composition, aluminum cools quickly and must have heat added to maintain a constant temperature for longer periods of time. The lid should not be preheated over campfire flames due to danger of cracking.

Baking

The best fuel for a D.O. is either coals directly from the fire or commercially-made charcoal briquettes are more convenient and predictable. They may be heated with lighter fluid or on top of a campfire grill. Briquettes are ready to use when they start to color gray.

Some handy tools for making the transfer of hot coals includes a pair of leather gloves, a shovel, tongs and a pair of pliers for handling the D.O. and lifting the lid.

For a 12-inch D.O., evenly space 7 briquettes under the bottom (if your model does not have legs, use rocks and space 2-inches high), and again space 14 briquettes around the top lip, with a couple in the center. This arrangement should produce approximately 375-degrees F. If baking for longer than 30 minutes, add a few coals/briquettes to maintain temperature. When you bake in a D.O., the temperature inside the pot is affected by the temperature and air movement around it. To get relatively consistent baking results, some kind of windscreen will help—and even a reflective cover like a large stainless steel bowl positioned over the top will improve the efficiency.

Judging when your baking is done requires a balance of timing, instinct and a sense of smell. Breads and cakes will clearly have that "baked" aroma when done. Less predictable dishes can be checked by lifting the edge of the lid for a peek, or test with a knife blade or stick.

Jim Moore's Homestead

Jim Moore came to the Salmon River canyon in 1897 as a young man about 30 years of age. The gold strike was just starting at Thunder Mountain, but Jim chose to stay and settle on the north bank of the river, where the miners passed through on their way to use Campbell's Ferry. He sold vegetables, fruits, beef and hides to the Thunder Mountain traffic.

Moore held the ground as a mining claim and was required to use all fallen trees toward that purpose. As the flat was cleared, the hand-hewn timbers became useful buildings. Over a period of 15 years Jim constructed 9 different log cabins, each with a specific purpose. There was the main living cabin with adjacent root cellar, a blacksmith shop, chicken coop, and two-story barn.

The large field was irrigated by a side creek that was channeled through a log flume. Moore established an orchard with apples, pears and plums. There was also a large garden and hay field.

It was known that Moore operated a still to produce whiskey and peach brandy. His pistols and rifle were at the ready for anyone too interested in its location. A favorite mare was his watchdog and Jim rewarded her with baked biscuits.

Other than the 15 mile trip to Dixie for supplies, he never ventured far from his riverside home. Jim Moore was about 70 years old when he died in 1942. His cabins are still intact and pay tribute to his pioneer spirit.

Jim Moore's Homestead

Tolo's Heroic Ride on William Rhett's Steed

The clearing with buildings upriver from Rhett Creek, not far from Lemhi Bar, once belonged to William Rhett. Rhett was active in the early gold rushes of Florence and Warren, and also fought the Nez Perce when they raided settlements further on down the river.

Rhett's biggest claim to fame, however, was being owner of the steed which carried Tolo on her heroic ride to save the settlers of Slate Creek.

It was at the beginning of the Indian War of 1877. Word spread among the settlers living along the Salmon River that atrocities were being committed by some of Chief White Bird's men. Approximately thirty families, some from as far away as twenty miles, came to Slate Creek where a stockade was being built. There were forty women and children and only twenty-three men, William Rhett among them, poorly armed with a few breech-loaders and an old muzzle-loader.

The hostile Nez Perce were well-armed with Sharps, Winchesters, Remingtons and Springfields obtained from the Crow Indians who had negotiated deals with some lawless buffalo hunters from Montana.

Among the occupants of the hastily constructed barricade was a Nez Perce woman named Aleblemot. Because of her love of gambling, she was better known as Tolo, Chinook jargon for "wager." It was probably this love of betting that brought Tolo into such intimate contact with the white settlers. She spent a great deal of time in Florence and Slate Creek where gambling, for many, was a way of life. When she heard news of trouble, she went to her settler friends at Slate Creek.

The situation with the hostiles became more and more threatening as small bands of Nez Perce began to congregate at a camp within sight of the stockade. Help was needed—the closest source being the mining camp of Florence, twenty-six miles up the rugged mountain terrain. Yet, no man could be spared to make the ride.

Tolo volunteered to go. William Rhett stepped forth with a well-muscled steed and offered it to Tolo. Rhett didn't know to whom the horse belonged, but there was no doubt that it ws the best piece of horse-flesh within sight and could survive the strenuous ride ahead. Before Tolo loped off into the dusk, Rhett cautioned her to let no harm come to the animal.

Within minutes the horse lathered as it strained up the mountain-side at the urging of the sharp-heeled Tolo. A quarter moon barely lit the way as coyotes and hoot owls filled the darkness with night calls. Hours dragged by as the scent of pine woods and sweat gave way to the grassy fragrance of high mountain meadows—and sweat.

At Florence saloon keepers were turning down the kerosene lamps, wiping booze off the bars, and sweeping out dried mud tracked in by numerous pairs of boots. They were stopped at their tasks by the sound of hoof-beats hitting the hard-packed surface of the road.

As the sweat-drenched steed shuddered with exhaustion, the weary rider spread the alarm to the sleepy-eyed miners. Within thirty minutes a group was mounted and armed, ready to follow Tolo back down the mountain.

Just as dawn was breaking, the reinforcements arrived at Slate Creek. Much ado was made of Tolo and her heroic ride.

William Rhett rushed to examine the steed and as he ran his hands over the quivering horse, it dropped dead at Rhett's feet.

A settler stepped forth and inquired as to who had given the horse to the Indian woman for the ride. All eyes turned to Rhettt. After some verbal exchange, the price was settled and Rhett was coerced into paying the man $150 for the dead horse—thus becoming the owner of the steed which carried the red heroine who saved the day at Slate Creek.

Did Ya Hear? Painter's Got Some Cattle for Sale.

Just a ways up from MacKay Bar is the old J.R. Painter place, which was originally owned by E.O. Eakin.

J.R., an orphan adopted and reared by a wealthy family from New York, had heard as a young man of the trophy mountain sheep, elk, bear and moose which thrived in the canyonlands through which the Salmon River flowed in a place called Idaho. So he ventured West, hired Captain Guleke to boat him through the canyon and ended up buying the Eakin place. J.R. built a hunting lodge which he named "The Bungalow," complete with French windows, a trophy room and pool table—all which Guleke ferried downriver 150 miles from Salmon.

Besides trophy hunting, J.R. tried his hand at mining, growing fruit trees and raising hogs. He even imported a small herd of Jersey cattle. But that didn't turn out too well.

The cattle thrived on the grasses which grew along the steep slopes surrounding J.R.'s establishment, but with his fingers in so many pies, Painter didn't have much time to tend his increasing herd. The Jerseys grew strong and wild roaming the slopes—even a seasoned cowhand would have had difficulty rounding them up.

One day in early August, Painter sized the cattle situation up and decided that it was time to sell his herd. He realized the difficulty a buyer would encounter in moving the wild herd, so being a fair man, he set his price low.

Now down in Boise Valley lived a portly buyer who prided himself on buying cattle at rock-bottom prices. When he heard of Painter's low offer he hastened to close in on the deal. He took the first mail stage from Boise Valley to Warren.

The stage trail along the snaking Payette River was worrisome and poorly maintained. The nauseating, jostling, swaying of the coach on rusting springs did not set well with the man. The August heat caused sweat to run down the cattle buyer's brow, drip off his nose and collect in little reservoirs in the folds of his chins. Yet, the sweet cattle deal was foremost in his mind and he appeased himself by rubbing his hands together in anticipation and taking deep draws on his fat cigar.

He arrived in Warren eager to rent a mount and continue on his way. But there were no horses to be had at Warren. In the spirit of adventure, the big man struck out for the South Fork of the Salmon afoot, for surely a horse would be found at the Dustin Ranch. His fee seemed to swell in his boots as he walked, certain that the Dustin Ranch lay just over the rise—well maybe the next rise, then. The man limped twelve long miles.

But there were no horses at the Dustin Ranch. The befuddled buyer bedded down for the night. The next morning, fresh from a sound night's sleep, he pondered his situation. Warren was twelve foot-weary miles back. The Frank Smith place was but 5½ miles ahead. Certainly a horse would be available at the Smith place. But the hills grew steeper, the sun grew hotter, rattlesnakes buzzed among the boulders and it took the poor portly man an entire day to cover the 5½ miles. The occupants of the Smith place took pity on the man. He was fed and given a bed. The next morning he was taken, astride a horse, to Smith's Saddle. But from there he had to walk on down to Andy Nelson's place. He arrived suffering from exhaustion and sunstroke.

Luther Perkins happened to be staying at the Nelson place, so he fed the suffering man, fixed him a place to sleep—and said how sorry he was that he had no horse to spare.

The next day the cattle buyer hitched up his bagging trousers and limped on down to MacKay Bar where he was ferried across the river in a boat. That day he made it as far as Bill Jackson's.

Now Bill Jackson was a colorful old coot who lived in a hole gouged in the bank with a couple of logs for support. He could size up a person in a glance and if he liked someone he'd lay down his life. But if he didn't—well...

The greedy cattle buyer found Bill Jackson unfriendly,

but he was tired and it was getting dark, so he dared not venture on. The prospector sat tight-lipped and frowning as the stranger siddled up to the campfire sniffing at the chow simmering in a suspended kettle. That was all he got for supper—a sniff. And the next morning he sat bleary-eyed as Jackson polished off the contents of the kettle for breakfast. So, without as much as an ort to quiet his rumbling stomach, the eager cattle buyer hurried on to J.R. Painter's ranch.

He hastened up to the door and gave it a hearty, self-assured rap. J.R. Painter came to the door, whereby the buyer introduced himself. Without inviting the gent in, J.R. pointed up the steep hillsides toward Lemhi Creek, said he'd talk with the buyer at two o'clock the next day after the cattle had been viewed, closed the door and returned to his den.

The buyer stood looking at the closed door for a long while, his stomach growling and his pants bagging. Slowly he turned his gaze to the steep hillsides. His eyes climbed up, up—through brush, over boulders—up towards the robin's egg blue sky until, near the very very top they came to rest on tiny moving specks. Were they the cattle? Range horses? A herd of elk, perhaps? Whatever they were, the man never found out. He merely turned away and started hobbling back to Warren. The return trek took him seven long, sweltering days.

Treasured Recipes from Early Settlers Along the Salmon River

Maggie's Bean Dumplings

> *4 cups cornmeal*
> *½ tsp. soda*
> *2 cups cooked dried beans, drained*
> *2 cups boiling water*

Put cornmeal in bowl, mix in beans. Hollow out a hole and put in soda and water. Make dough stiff enough to form balls. Drop balls into kettle of boiling water. Cook about 35 minutes. Serve with cooked greens (such as Shepherd's Purse, purslane, dock or nettle) and chunks of venison or mountain sheep.

Ella's Ash Cake

> *2 cups cornmeal*
> *tsp. baking soda*
> *1 cup fresh buttermilk*
> *⅓ cup fat*

Add enough water to make thick dough when mixed with above. Salt to taste. Make a hole in center of ashes of hot fire. Rake ashes down to hearth. Place dough in hole. Let it crust over then cover with hot ashes and embers. Bake for an hour.

Viola's Sweet Corn Pudding

10 to 12 ears sweet corn	*2 Tbsp. flour*
1½ Tbsp. sugar	*1 Tbsp. butter*
1 qt. fresh cow's milk	*3 brown chicken eggs*

Grate corn and mix with milk. Add salt if you have a mind to. Work flour and butter until creamy, then beat in sugar and egg yolks. Beat egg whites and put into corn and milk mixture. Bake in hot oven. If you like it sweeter, add sugar and cream.

Mr. Smith's Leather Breeches

Break fresh green beans and string on a thread, hang in the sun or by the warm stove to dry. To prepare them they need to be parboiled, rinsed, removed from thread and cooked with a good-sized chunk of salt pork.

Babe's Dandelion Greens

They can be picked until they bloom. Pick over carefully the tender young greens. Wash in saltwater and rinse in several waters. Put in boiling water with a piece of salt pork or bacon. Boil one hour. Drain well, add salt and boil another hour. When well done and tender, drain and eat with fresh butter.

Emma's Venison Roast

Select a four to six-pound boneless roast and slit it up the sides and top at three-inch intervals. Stuff slits with piecs of chopped onion and garlic. Salt and pepper the roast. Put in pot and pour in enough vinegar to cover meat. Let stand 12 hours or more. Lift out meat, coat with flour and lard and brown on all sides quickly. Pour on some of the vinegar, cover and cook 2 hours.

"Guntower"

Last of the Mountain Men

In 1929, with an oncoming Depression, Sylvan Hart responded by looking for a place that had the natural resources to defeat it. "I could not have found a better place than the Salmon River. I spent some $50 a year then for what little I needed to buy." Armed with a rifle, an ax, a few staples, and a master's degree in engineering, Sylvan chose a riverside bar on Five Mile Creek. "I always had a garden and it was easy to get fruit and I made moccasins and clothing out of animal skins," recalled Hart, who soon became known as "Buckskin Bill."

"It was the custom of my family, going back about 300 years, for the young men to stay in the woods for at least a year. I just liked it so well I never came out." During his lifetime, Sylvan constructed several stucco-covered buildings with hand-hewn timbers. To complete his library room, Hart packed in, on his back, the plexiglass cockpit from a B-18 aircraft, that served as a reading alcove. The individual cabins included a kitchen, bedroom and workshop with a sign reading "Blacksmithing & Millinery." This is where Sylvan forged copper and steel to produce eating utensils, ladles, knives, kettles and other cooking pots. Many of the items had to be preceded with the building of a specialty tool.

When it came to guns, Sylvan believed that no mountaineer was worth anything unless he kept at least 15 guns in his house. To help meet this quota he made many of his own flintlock rifles, boring them on an ingenious handmade machine, plus manufacturing his own molds for bullets. "You know, if you can make a really good gun, and do all the work, you don't worry about breaking it. There's some satisfaction having a gun the way you want it. With a flintlock, too, you can shoot a long time without depending upon anybody else. If you've got the powder."

One beautifully handmade rifle attracted the attention of

"Buckskin Bill" and forged copperwork

First Census of Idaho Territory

Idaho County	Voters	Non-voters	Females	Children
Florence	430	145	—-	—-
Warren's Diggings	420	240	—-	—-
Slate Creek	160	50	4	2
Long Bar	70	80	—-	—-
Total	1080	515	4	2

a wealthy businessman who offered Hart $500 for it and was turned down. Then $1,000 and finally a blank check to fill out for whatever he wanted, saying, "You do use money, don't you?" "No," said Sylvan, "not where I live."

Animals like elk, deer, big-horn sheep, bear and cougars were plentiful in the area Sylvan lived, but he never killed an animal around his place, unless it was clearly a case of destructive trespassing, like the bear that broke into his root-cellar.

Deer and elk hide was a popular clothing with Hart. It protected him from thorns, and the fringed edge let water run off faster. "I'm afraid of one thing—a cold wind," claimed Sylvan, "A cold wind is what kills you in the mountains, but it can't cut through a big stag hide." Also popular with Sylvan was his bear-hide hat, modeled after a Spanish Conquistador helmet.

The meat from these animals was a major source of food for Hart. "Animals that eat other animals have light meat. Animals that eat grass have dark meat."

Next to his home, and irrigated by Five Mile Creek, was a 10,000 square-foot garden that produced asparagus, parsnips, carrots, beets, cabbage, corn, squash, cucumbers, cantaloupe, strawberries, rhubarb, peppers, onions, garlic, horseradish, beans and potatoes. Fruit trees were planted at the edge and included peaches, pears, apples and apricots. Breads and cakes were made with different wheats grown and ground on the place, and Sylvan was particularly fond of sourdough concoctions. "Every country has some food that is positively rotten and is positive that you'd like some of it. In this country we have rotten sourdough."

A final monument to Sylvan's artistry and skill was the "Guntower" he built in the '60s after the U.S. Forest Service got the notion they should evict Hart from the Idaho Primitive Area. It was complete with gunports and all the supplies to "take a stand." The situation was resolved when the Forest Service discovered it didn't even own the bar—and it was part of a patented mine upstream. Hart's nephew was able to obtain the title and in 1974 gave Sylvan a deed to his home.

Even though Sylvan chose to live in this remote wilderness, he did not consider himself a hermit. Hart made occasional trips to Burgdorf (population 6) some 40 miles away, where he purchased powder, books and tea, all paid for with panned gold. During World War II, he became a toolmaker at the Boeing factory in Kansas and helped the military develop systems for bombsights and autopilots.

When questioned about the Air Force jets that sometimes rattle the wilderness with sonic booms, Sylvan said, "Better to listen to sonic booms that eat fish heads and rice with chopsticks in a few years."

Sylvan had his philosophy about city people too. "They hurry and rush all the really important things. When I'm finished making a gun, for instance, I set it back aside for awhile. I may not test it or fire it for weeks. That's what the city does to people. They're so anxious to complete anything that they never plan it out properly or enjoy it right when it's finished. "For the city man, life is just a jumble, like the facts in a college freshman's notebook. But you can ask me about nearly anything, and I can answer because I've had time to think about it."

Hart had time to relax and enjoy life. "I work three, four hours before it gets hot, then maybe two more after the sun goes down," said Sylvan. "If you lived in a place like this and had to work hard eight hours a day, you'd be a pitiful incompetent."

Sylvan may have been the last man to live out such a lifestyle in the Idaho wilderness. When his burial took place on Five Mile Bar, three friends fired a salute with Hart's own long rifles. The granite tombstone reads:

Sylvan A. Hart

"Buckskin Bill"

May 10, 1906—April 29, 1980

The Last of the Mountain Men

Moonshine from Mountain Stills

It was a low blow—legislature constituted Idaho a prohibition district effective January 1, 1916. Depression quickly set in as saloons in Salmon, Riggins, Warren and Dixie began serving lemonade, or the nauseatingly "zippy" soft drink cruely labeled Beerette. Some saloon keepers, unable to look their patrons in the eye as they slid "a regular man's drink—vigorous, wholesome, refreshing, clean and sparkling "Becco"' across the booze-stained bar, simply closed their doors. Forever.

And what of their patrons? Miners, who lived in tents or rustic one-room cabins, no longer had the lively, brightly-lit, music-filled saloons to occupy their long, dreary evenings. Men from the pack-trains and freight wagons found little solace in lemonade after their long treks into the back country. It just didn't cut the dust like a mug of cold, frothy beer or a quick shot of whiskey. The people of the Salmon River area went into deep brooding.

To save the rugged Salmon River Country from drying up, heroic bootleggers set up stills. Along with moonshine, applejack, wine and home-made beer soon abounded. Most folks made their own refreshments, but some didn't have the skill or patience, so purchased theirs instead. It wasn't hard to get the stuff, but some of the stuff was, well, just plain "hard."

There was the stuff Sheepherder Bill from Porphyry Creek way made. It was a prune mash concoction that could grow hair on a lizard. But Bill's still blew up, and Bill and his cabin went with it.

Then there was the stuff Lava Pete and Chance Michsel made. The two were from Hell's Canyon Country and would bring their "pizen moonshine" to the Salmon River folks when the Snake River folks had had their fill. The uncouth pair got the sugar for their enterprise from Old Crazy Sugar. It was believed that it was Old Crazy's sugar that made the moonshine so rot-gut.

Old Crazy Sugar with Hex and Het

Old Crazy lived among the jagged mountains near Seven Devils with two goats who shared his burlap pallet. He not only smelled of goat, but shared the fleas which thrived among his scraggly gray chest hairs. The old man looked at the world through lifeless eyes, red-rimmed along sagging lower lids. His hair lay matted to his head and his long mustache frequently bore food particles. Nothing seemed to affect the man much, except the sight of sugar, whereby Old Crazy Sugar would suck the mustache into his mouth and begin vacuuming it noisily. The crazy old man had an affinity for sugar and cunning methods of acquiring it.

When folks saw Old Crazy Sugar coming towards their cabins, flanked by his goats, Hex and Het, they'd hide their sugar and sweets. Those who took pity on the crazed fellow, relinquishing their sweets, often found the red-eyed nuisance and his goat duo taking up residency in their yards.

Because of his persistence, Old Crazy Sugar managed to lay claim to quite a stash of sugar each year—tins and tins of it, which he buried for safekeeping. Yet, his affinity for the stuff was so great that he frequently dug the tins up and sifted the priceless crystals through unwashed fingers, over and over again. Eventually the sparkling sugar crystals became grimy and gray.

When moonshine season came around, Lava and Chance would pay a visit on Old Crazy Sugar. They'd get the old man and his goats drunk on last season's moonshine, then dig up the stashes of gray, gritty sweetener for their next season's batch.

It was pure "pizen moonshine" all right, and testament to the hale internal constitution of the Salmon and Snake River folk.

Genius of the Salmon River

Bill Jackson arrived in the Salmon River canyon around 1916, carrying basic supplies and a few handmade tools. He was about 41 years of age. With plans to spend the winter gold mining, Bill constructed a raft for floating downriver.

Jackson cut an impressive figure of a man. Standing over 6' 3", he was broad-chested with dark hair and a handlebar mustache. His past history told of working as a seaman, a north woods logger, and a Pennyslvania iron worker.

His genius as an engineer quickly spread as Bill traveled up and down the canyon inventing and fixing, designing irrigation systems, and mining. It wasn't known if he had formal training as an engineer, but Jackson clearly showed an intuitive ability as a mechanical genius. His three-dimensional mind demonstrated skills of a man ahead of his time. From the most basic materials Bill produced original machinery—that worked with efficiency.

Living about three miles above the South Fork confluence, Jackson Bar bears the name of this early pioneer. Bill's shelter was as simple as his inventions were complicated. A few logs supporting the roof of a hole dug out of the bank was all he required. When the nights grew cold, Bill's fire simply grew larger.

Water from side canyon creeks or the Salmon River was Jackson's favorite power source, and the most available. He used it to run sawmills wherever he went. One job required a hole through a metal blade, and without a drill, Bill shot the center out with his rifle. Another project was a water-powered stamp mill for the Painter Bar Mine. Many of his machines were a mystery to those who saw them, but all agreed how well they worked.

On occasional trips to town, Jackson would get drunk as the next man, but returning to the canyon, he again pursued his complicated projects. Bill's generosity in constructing these inventions was based on friendship, not

Bill Jackson

compensation. He was seldom paid for his mills and was most often broke, but still optimistic about life.

In his later years, Bill was called upon to build a sawmill and irrigation pipeline for a recently acquired ranch. The owner bought a new trailer as living quarters for Jackson. He decided the interior arrangement wasn't suited for his style, so he removed the furniture and partitions, making his bed on the floor.

The one luxury Jackson allowed himself, a Ford tractor, proved to be his undoing. In 1962, returning from a funeral along the Salmon River road, Bill drove off into the river. The character of Bill Jackson might best be summed up by the memory, he was always doing nice things for people—if he liked them.

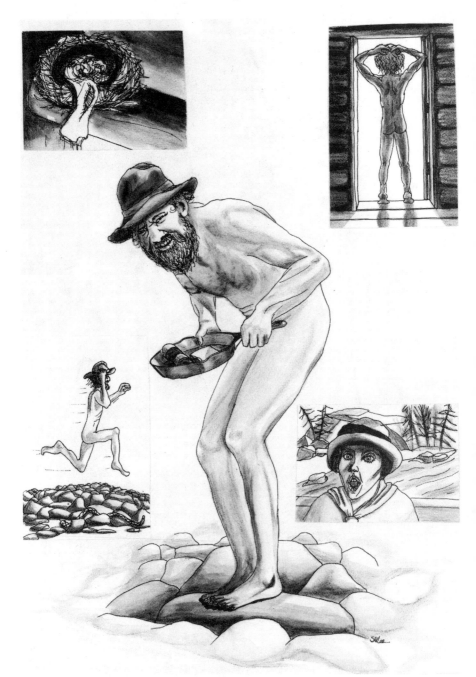

Day in the Life of a Miner

A Day in the Life of a Miner
Early 1900s

A canyon wren warbled. The bearded invader of the banks of the river awakened. He rose up and banged his head on a rough hewn board on the top bunk. As he picked slivers from the top of his balding head, he surveyed the rudely structured room with red-eyed indifference.

Where were his socks?

He searched among the provisions in the vacant space beneath his lower bunk. He looked under the mattress of fir boughs covered with worn Pendleton blankets. He rattled through the dry goods box nailed to the wall where cooking utensils and a spare pair of long-handled underwear mingled with a rasher of bacon. He rifled through the piles of books and old papers littering the crude table by the fireplace. Eventually the man tender-footed his way across the whip-sawn floor boards, swung wide the door and squinted at the sky.

It was going to be a scorcher. Rattlers would be shading themselves in the shadow of every rock, branch or clump of grass. But what the hell. He had staked a placer claim at Whiskey Gulch and he was going to tear the place to pieces in his mad search for gold—socks or no.

He shucked out of his sleeping johns and stood in his all-togethers, grinning at the thought of some hapless maiden floating the river and seeing him standing in the doorway—of her swooning from the boat and being swallowed whole by a sturgeon. The thought pleased him. He would merely tip his hat to bid the lady farewell.

Hat. He tenderfooted his way back into the cabin and snatched up his hat. He slapped the broad-brimmed, slouched felt over the shiny dome fringed by his shaggy growth of uncut hair. And he stood thus in the doorway, naked from feet to neck, but well-clothed above.

But should he be seen in all his glory down on the bar, sitting on the driftwood log, calmly sipping coffee, would the shock not be greater yet? Might a tender lass faint dead away at the sight?

So he hobbled across the pebbly stretch of ground, coffee tin and pot in hand, to the fire pit by the driftwood log on the bar. He sat within full view of the river—the first prominent sight a boatman would see upon rounding the bend.

He drank a lot of coffee—two potfuls, to be exact. Nature called. The sun had been hitting the sand so the miner had to hot-foot his way across thirty yards of it to a large clump of bushes where there was sufficient cover to water his horse with modesty.

Before he returned to the bar he made his way back to the cabin for some bacon from the rasher, a tin of beans and a skillet. Back on the bar he fixed himself a fine meal, the same monotonous stuff he'd been eating for months. But on this day it was fine—because at any minute a boat could round the bend and a lady could be seated within. The shock would be so great that the wide-eyed stare would freeze on her face, forever. And he, the miner, would be immortalized in that frozen stare!

The heat beat down and the man, with belly filled, grew drowsy and slumped across the log. The sun did such a fine job of painting him red, that when a blunt object jabbed him, he startled with a yell of pain.

A black bear had nosed him while investigating the source of the scent of bacon. It became frightened by the sudden movements of the man, reared up, then gave chase. The miner limbered his sunburned flesh by running as fast as he could, leaping clear of several rattlers who were heading toward the river to drink.

The bear was fast, but the miner was faster, barefooting it across the stones. He made it to the cabin and slammed the door, bloodying the nose of the bear. Then he hooted and hollered in glee as he picked burrs from between his toes! He couldn't remember when he'd had a livelier day, or a day so imaginatively filled! He jigged across the bare-boarded floor and sang a brawdy tune! He threw back his head to laugh aloud and stopped short.

There in the rafter was a pack rat's nest trailing a mangled toe. He positioned the table and climbed atop to have a closer look. There, nestled amid the shreds of his socks, were five hairless baby pack rats.

The sight spoiled his whole damned day.

Polly "Lalu Nathoy" Bemis

Lalu Nathoy was born in China, September 11, 1853, to a family of farmers. A lengthy drought that led to starvation forced her father to sell Lalu into slavery to get seeds for his crops. She was put on a ship for Portland and upon arrival, purchased by a Chinese man for $2,500. He then took her to the town of Warren, about 12 miles up Warren Creek from the Salmon River.

Her new owner, Hong King, put Lalu to work in his saloon. She quickly gained popularity and was given the name "Polly." A resident of Warren remembers "Polly was a good woman and entitled to a great deal of consideration because of her upright conduct in rather difficult circumstances." Though her basic needs were taken care of by Hong King, Polly's greatest desire was for freedom.

To gain money for buying back her indentured servant contract, Polly would pan the sweepings from the saloon floor each night to recover the spilled gold dust. When she finally approached the old Chinese man, he said he would never sell at any price.

One of Polly's many friends was Charlie Bemis, who ran a saloon and enjoyed gambling. In a poker game with Hong King, Bemis raised the bet so high that Hong was forced to put Polly's contract in the pot. Bemis won the hand and Polly was given her freedom. With Charlie's help, Polly started a boarding house and life in Warren seemed to be moving along smoothly.

Then on the morning of September 16, 1890, Bemis found himself confronted with a mad half-Indian who lost

Bemis Ranch

$250 to him in a card game the night before. "Give me back $150. You've got until I finish rollin' this cigarette, then I'll shoot your eye out." Charlie misjudged the threat as a bluff and the man fired, missing his eye but shattering his cheek.

The doctor was called from Grangeville and succeeded in only removing half the bullet, leaving Bemis with the likelihood of a slow death from lead poisoning. Days later and showing no signs of improvement, Polly discovered a lump at the back of Charlie's head. An incision was made by Polly who found and removed the other half of the bullet. Charlie's life was saved as Polly nursed him back to health. (Nine days after the shooting, Bemis' assailant was tracked down, arrested, and sentenced to five years in prison).

A new threat to Polly was the U.S. Immigration Department that had the power to deport her to China, so on August 13, 1894, Charlie Bemis married Polly. It was just a short while later they decided to move to the Salmon River.

At last Polly was back to the life she loved as a young girl in China. Their new home quickly blossomed with a productive garden and orchard including mullberry and chestnut trees, plus ducks, chickens and a cow. As she worked in the garden, Polly collected worms for the afternoon's fishing. Catching Charlie laying down to watch an anthill, she told him, "If you'd work'um like ants we no be poor folks." Though Bemis made occasional trips back to Warren, Polly preferred to stay in the canyon. Her friends could come visit her there.

In August of 1922, the cabin caught fire and burned to the ground. Charlie had become an invalid and was barely saved with the help of Charlie Shepp, a rancher across the river. He died two months later, and Polly made plans to live in Warren.

Polly's return was quite a celebration. At 70 years old, she was taken on her first automobile ride to Grangeville. There she saw her first motion picture show and her first train. Later trips took Polly to Boise to see more modern wonders. All this was fine for a visit, but she yearned for her life on the river.

An agreement was made with Charlie Shepp and Pete Klinkhammer who ranched across the river from her home. They would build her a new cabin and in exchange she would leave the place to them. Polly again lived happily on the banks of the Salmon until 1933, when she became ill and was taken to the hospital in Grangeville. When told by the nurse she would get well again, Polly replied, "No, me too old to get well, me have to go to other world to get well."

Polly "Lalu Nathoy" Bemis died November 6, 1933, and though she wanted to be buried alongside Charlie Bemis as the river, she was laid to rest in Grangeville. Then in 1987, a group of historians arranged to have her remains relocated to her beloved homestead. Polly Bemis was finally home for good.

The First Winter in Florence

North of the Salmon, five miles up the trail by the Wind River Pack Bridge, once lay the astonishingly rich placer camp of Florence, discovered in the autumn of 1861, by a party of California prospectors. The Florence placers were the most picturesque and superficially the richest of all the famed Idaho camps. The town, named after a store and innkeeper's daughter, was situated near the center of a basin resembling a gigantic inverted satellite dish. The basin is surrounded by a chain of forbidding snow-capped mountains.

News of the riches spread swiftly and a strange and motley group of prospectors rushed across swollen rivers, scrambled over rugged mountains, and tiptoed through Indian-infested country in search of the camp of Florence, 6,000 feet above sea level.

By November, nearly 2,000 men had found the way. A ramshackled settlement was slapped together. Some housing was made of poles and chinking of mud, some of whipsawed lumber from nearby forests, and some merely canvas tents. All expected to become rich. None expected to ride out the coldest, most miserable winter in the history of Idaho.

On December 21, "Doc" Noble started out from Pierce City with a few pack horses loaded with supplies. For ten days the pack string labored through snow drifts and fought freezing temperatures to cover the 125 miles to Florence. A small group of Nez Perce took pity on "Doc" and helped him reach his destination.

"Doc" Noble found the settlement troubled and made note of the following incidents: "...I saw a young man with emaciated frame and ghastly countenance picking up something off a pile of snow and eating it with great relish. On stepping up to him, I found that in a famishing condition, he had chanced to come on a spot or bank of snow on which some kitchen slop containing a few cooked beans had lately been thrown out from an adjoining shanty, and these he was picking up and devouring with great avidity. I gave him five dollars, which he eagerly but thankfully clutched, and went to a store, and paid it all for

First Winter in Florence

two and a half pounds of flour. He was a stranger without friends and wasted to a mere skeleton by wanting and destitution. He is now employed in packing on his back from the Mountain House, and a few days since he packed a hundred pounds of bacon on his back from there into town—more than fifteen miles over rough trail.

"One day a man called at the cabin where I stayed and in subdued tones asked, 'What chance can a fellow have of getting that cow's head lying on the roof?' which he said 'might do to cook when a fellow's hungry and has nothing to eat.' He got it willingly. It had been lying there four months, but most of the time covered with snow."

By late January, the only food available was flour, which sold for two dollars per pound. Famine was rampant. Hundreds of men were living on gruel made of melted snow water and flour which they washed down with bitter pine needle tea.

Snow drifts were twelve feet high and men had to tunnel from one place to another. They warmed water with which to operate their rockers and dug beneath the snow to the frozen earth in order to wash out enough gold to pay for the flour they ate. Snow blindness plagued many of the miners and they blackened their faces with pulverized charcoal and grease to help protect themselves from the glare. As the winter dragged on, prospectors sat in windowless cabins or frigid tents lit by flickering candlelight. If they were fortunate, a piece of damp wood provided weak heat. But, because of the deep snow, wood was as scarce as food, so few enjoyed the luxury of warmth.

During that winter, several miners found an unconscious, nearly starved, half-frozen prospector lying on a trail near Florence. His name was Charles Leopold Ostner, an honor art student from the University of Heidelberg. He had become lost from his party during a blizzard and had wandered the wilds for nearly a month.

The poor fellow survived under the care of the miners. He was so grateful that he promised the town a gift derived from his artistic abilities. A huge mound of snow was piled in the center of the street and water was poured upon it until the mound became ice. A large canvas was then draped over the ice. For days Charles Leopold Ostner worked beneath the canvas with hammer and chisel. When the canvas was drawn away, the townfold of Florence viewed what was probably Idaho's first ice sculpture—General George Washington astride his horse.

Somehow the prospectors drew strength from Ostner's sculpture. It reminded them of the General's ride through Valley Forge on a frightful winter's day. And if George could muster up the fight for his country, certainly the miners could battle Idaho's winter for the gold. And they did!

Charles Leopold Ostner's Ice Sculpture

Big Tom

Ode to Big Tom

As a spotted kitten he scampered along,
    on paws four sizes too big,
Searching for morsels of many sorts
    for he had the appetite of a pig.
He munched on snails, rodents and crows
    and even wolfed down a few frogs
But he didn't know taste until he sampled
    three of Coony's hound dogs.

The kitten soon grew to a slender-bodied cat
    with powerful legs and jaws.
His appetite grew and became quite pronounced—
    but then everything has its flaws.
He prowled the canyons of the Salmon River,
    the saddles, gulches and flats.
He prowled with poise and he prowled with pride,
    Big Tom was the king of cats.

Up on Johnson Saddle a man called Vern
    sang a woeful song.
He said one night Big Tom came around—
    next morning his goats were gone.
And on Indian Creek Ranch a man called Matt
    said his wife was in a prattle,
Two nights before some big tawny cat had eaten
    a milch cow and some cattle.

Down by Sweet Anise Spring old man Jordon was
    wailing and singing the blues.
It was tough enough to lose one's stock,
    but the scourge ate his critters by twos!
Yet, down at Mammoth Star Mine prospector Bob
    had no reason to whine.
The stealthy beast had entered camp and devoured
    a dozen porcupine.

A reward was posted for the connoisseur cougar
    and hunters came from afar
They told tall tales of their fearless deeds
    and hung around the bar.
They shot up the town, tempted the ladies,
    and swaggered up the street,
While Big Tom roamed the hillsides
    looking for something to eat.

And food he found! The Salmon country was a cornucopia
    of good eating.
There were cows and mules; and the sheep he swallowed
    as they were bleating.
There were tender horses and hogs; chickens and dogs;
    and if that were not enough,
There were elk and deer and bear and moose, but Tom
    found them to be quite tough.

The reward money doubled, then tripled and another
    thousand was added to that.
All of a sudden serious tracking began—
    it was a hefty sum for a cat!
The hillsides and the canyons swarmed with armed men
    all eager to get rich.
Big Tom knew he'd been had so he turned himself in
    and dropped with nary a twitch.

                              by Darcy Williamson

Idaho County Free Press, January 25, 1923: *"'Big Tom,' a
200 pound cougar, was killed last week along the breaks of
the Salmon. For more than three years stockmen devoted
much time to hunting this elusive predator, claimed
responsible for the loss of hundreds of sheep and cattle."*

Testimonials

"You can't imagine (maybe you can) how damned difficult it's been to concentrate on anything since we left Idaho. Can't get that blooming river or the gorgeous scenery out of my mind...the magnificent weather...the peace and solitude...and the good times.

"What I'm trying to say is thank you for a truly memorable experience. The food, the people, the way you take care of everyone and everything including keeping our gear dry—it was all superb."

Maggie Kennedy, Dallas, Texas

"Outdoor camping has never been so comfortable. Your custom-made overhead canopys, roomy dome tents, and camp chairs made any weather comfortable and enjoyable."

Vicki Milgrim, Breakaway Adventure Travel,
Cambridge, Mass.

"It is hard to imagine a better introduction to the sport. Moments of excitement alternate with long periods of serenity. A long float through majestic mountain landscapes makes the urban world and its cares seem far away. The following year we ran the Salmon again, and we were hooked."

Fryer Calhoun, *New West Magazine*

"'This isn't a white-water/white-knuckles type trip,' says Steven Shephard. The emphasis is on comfort and exceptionally good eating. Plus speciality trips featuring everything from wine tasting to photography workshops."

Harpers Bazaar

"Salmon River Outfitters offers what might just be the best river rafting adventure in America. Owner Steven Shephard guides every trip and meticulously plans the route on 80 miles of Idaho's beautiful Salmon River. The Salmon's main fork is ideal for recreation—deep, not too rocky, and peppered with rapids that are exciting but not too dangerous. The section you'll travel is sometimes heavily forested, sometimes bounded by steep rock walls, with bighorn sheep, river otters and eagles often spotted along the way. Salmon River Outfitters' attention to detail includes dedication to safety, relaxation, comfortable camping and, most important, food."

Travel & Leisure

"Steven Shephard's Salmon River Outfitters has elevated camping to a fine art. They provide everything but your clothes and personal items."

Los Angeles Times

"'Why should civilized people have to compromise the comforts of good living just because they're camping in the wilderness?' said Steven Shephard, whose company provides the opportunity to go downstream in upscale style."

The New York Times

"The Salmon River is unique. Spared from routine damming, it has carved the second deepest gorge in North America. Towering snow-capped mountains feed frequent side creeks into this evergreen canyon, where nature, thankfully, remains unrestrained."

Dallas Times Herald

Salmon River Prospector Proverbs

A friend remains a friend up to his pockets.

The worst wheel on the cart makes the most noise.

He that drinks his Applejack alone, let him catch his mule alone.

Before you run in double harness, look well to the other horse.

Fish and visitors stink after three days.

Poverty is no disgrace, but it is decidedly inconvenient.

He who has gold is a welcome guest.

Better go to bed supperless than to get up in debt.

Everyone lays his load on the willing horse.

Throw no dirt in the well that gives you water.

He must hunger in frost who will not work in the heat.

When the well is dry, one knows the worth of water.

You can't tell the depth of the well by the length of the handle on the pump.

Steal a horse, and you'll die without being ill.

He who would sell a blind horse praises his feet.

Man is the only animal that can be skinned more than once.

He that drinks fast pays slow.

There are more old drunkards than old doctors.

Bad breath is better than none at all.

It is a sorry dog who wants game but will not hunt for it.

Don't throw away the old bucket until you know if the new one holds water.

A foolish boatman looks one way and pulls the other.

Idaho's Salmon River

AAA-California State Automobile Association
Motorland Magazine—by Don Patton

Twenty-four years passed between my first and second dunkings in Idaho's Salmon River. But the Salmon hadn't changed—and neither, so far as I could tell, had Idaho. As I traversed the state by jet, small plane, bus and finally by raft, I saw a sparsely populated region with rugged mountains and fertile valleys, where horse and horsepower work side by side.

City dwellers who equate remote with uninhabitable will find the people are friendly, but the land is still as rough around the edges as it was when fur trappers and Indians were the only residents. It's a place of evocative names: Craters of the Moon, Hell's Canyon and Seven Devils, and amazingly contrasting topography: from some of the West's most irrigated farmland to its most inpenetrable mountains, from arid badlands in the south to dense forests in the north.

There's a 200 by 170 mile region in the middle of the state, anchored in the southwest by Boise and the northeast by Missoula, where road is the past tense of what you do with horses, and most visitors travel the old-fashioned ways: afoot, afloat or on horseback. There's not a paved road in this entire zillion acre expanse of the northern Rockies. Even Lewis and Clark, after starting through it, concluded that these mountains were too desolate and too difficult to traverse.

Centerpiece of this vast wilderness is the Salmon River, celebrated in film and brochure as the River of No Return. Steven Shephard, chief guide and owner of Salmon River Outfitters, hypothesized that the river got its name in the days when boatmen ferried supplies downriver on flatboats, and then broke up the boats to sell the boards at the end of the trip. What went down didn't come back.

The Salmon is no longer a serious threat to an experienced boatman. It is, however, a marvelous river for the serious tourist. As one of the West's great mountain rivers its 400 undammed miles offer constantly changing scenery that is richly imbedded with human history, and a trip back into the American West.

Guests of Salmon River Outfitters spend the first night at a remote riverside guest lodge about a quarter mile upstream from the put-in. A base camp for both pack and float trips, the lodge provides an easy transition from city life. We spent a lazy afternoon reading, swimming and chatting with fellow travelers. The following morning, after a ranch-style breakfast and one last look at indoor plumbing, we pushed off for five days and four nights in the wilderness.

Salmon whitewater, while claiming its share of inattentive boatmen and their cargo, won't inspire much fear in rafters after the first day or two, and most of the river, at least during midsummer flows, provides comfortable floating.

Drifting for six hours a day, soaking in sun and solitude, while stretched out on a raft tube, offers more varied views than a lounge chair and is almost as relaxing.

Those in search of greater excitement can find it in inflatable kayaks. Running my first rapid I flipped the kayak and the Salmon claimed my right tennis shoe. That was the worst casulty of the trip.

River trips feature near equal mixes of floating and shore

time. The Salmon provides numerous off-stream diver-
sions, including hot springs, Indian rock art and fishing.
The river has several species of trout as well as a steelhead
run, and while most of its human residents have cleared
out, the canyon is still home—and this is eyewitness
testimony—to bears, moose, bighorn sheep, eagles and
otters. The clear, cool waters of the river are also perfect for
swimming.

Camping on this trip was as far from roughing it as the
Salmon River is from anywhere. Campsites are sandy
beaches, swept clean by high water each spring and kept
clean by fastidious campers. The guides attend to setup
chores at each camp, freeing guests to fish, hike, read or
raid the hors d'oeuvres. The food that materialized from
Shephard's streamside ovens is first-rate. We were treated to
salmon, chicken enchiladas, banana buttermilk pancakes,
tuna stuffed tomatoes, shish kebab and other improbable
feasts that have earned mention in *Bon Appetit* and
Gourmet magazines.

Fine food, wildlife and whitewater aside, my lasting
impression of the Salmon is rooted in the past, not the
present. The river carried us into a land that has changed
little in 100 years, and it didn't take much imagination to
picture the pioneers, scratching out a living on the river's
banks.

What's remarkable about the canyon is that recent and
remote are so closely allied here. Until just a few years ago,
floaters could visit with Buckskin Bill, "last of the mountain
men," who built his house—and all the furniture, tools and
firearms that filled it. He lived much as other turn-of-the-
century settlers did, wrestling an uncomplicated life from a
land that killed some and drove most others around the
bend and back to town.

Jim Moore was another pioneer who came to the Salmon
in 1889, built a home, planted orchards and began trading
with miners bound for Thunder Mountain. He rarely left the
canyon before his death in 1942, and now he never will.
The nine log structures he built are being restored by
volunteers, using hand tools only, making this the most
interesting and complete historical site on the river.

Few other structures have survived their owners, but

stories have. The stories recount the hardships settlers endured to live here, and around every bend, history comes alive. Some of the tales are amusing, some grim, but this is a rugged land, and from great risks, come great rewards.

Bibliography

Beckoning the Bold, Rafe Gibbs, University of Idaho Press, 1976

Idaho Chinese Lore, Sister M. Alfreda Elsensohn, Idaho Corporation of Benedictine Sisters, 1979

Indian Legends from the Northern Rockies, Ella E. Clark, University of Oklahoma Press, 1966

The Last of the Mountain Men, Harold Peterson, Scribner, 1969

Lookout Wife, Jeanne Kellar Beaty, Random House, Inc., 1953

The Middle Fork and the Sheepeater War, Johnny Carrey, Backeddy Books, 1977

Pioneer Days in Idaho County, Volume 1 & 2, Sister M. Alfreda Elsensohn, Caxton, 1951

Polly Bemis, Sister M. Alfreda Elsensohn, Idaho Corporation of Benedictine Sisters, 1980

River of No Return, Johnny Carry and Cort Conley, Backeddy Books, 1978

Territorial Centennial Edition of the Idaho Almanac, 1963

Topping Out, Katherine Wonn Harris, Aldyth H. Logan, 1972

About the Authors and Artist

Darcy Williamson is an award winning writer from Central Idaho, with more than a dozen books to her credit including several all natural food cookbooks and a novel, *Sisters of a Different Dawn.*

Steven Shephard, owner and guide of Salmon River Outfitters has been a riverside chef since he began rafting the Salmon in 1972. His enthusiasm is expressed by retelling some favorite pioneer stories and sharing a few of his most popular recipes.

Shannon Dee is an artist whose outdoor skills have developed from living in several remote areas of New Zealand, including Fiordland (the Milford Track). This love of wild places led her to Idaho and the Salmon River where she now manages and guides with the Salmon River Outfitters year round.

SALMON RIVER OUTFITTERS

Steven Shephard and Shannon Dee spend their summers guiding river trips on Idaho's famous Salmon. Operating *Salmon River Outfitters*, they are committed to providing hassle-free vacations, with emphasis on convenience, comfort and cuisine.

Sharing this experience with other enthusiasts makes their profession a pleasure. Part of this enjoyment comes from personally designing the best equipment available, as well as planning an exceptional menu of delicious outdoor meals.

All 6-day trips start with the first afternoon/night at a remote riverside guestlodge. Then, at sandy riverside camps, all equipment is provided, including roomy dome tents, comfortable chairs, and everything for sleeping and dining.

Passengers may also choose among a variety of "Specialty Trips" like Indian Folklore & Native Foods, Photography Workshops, Wine Tasting, nightly Wilderness Guestlodge accomodations, and a professional Storyteller and Harpist.

Ten trips of limited size are conducted from June through September. For a brochure and more information, contact SRO, P. O. Box 307, Columbia, CA 95310 or telephone (209) 532-2766.

OTHER BOOKS BY DARCY WILLIAMSON

Sisters of a Different Dawn, a historical novel which takes place during the mid-1800s and deals with conflicts between a Boston-born woman and her Shoshoni sister-in-law. Set amid the dying fur era in Southeastern Idaho. $17.95, hardbound

Cooking with Spirit, North American Indian Food and Fact, co-authored with Lisa Railsback. Traditional and contemporary Native American cooking and the spiritual aspects of relating to that which nourishes our bodies, minds and souls. $12.95, perfect bound 8½ x 11

How to Prepare Common Wild Foods, covers wild foods of the mountains and valleys of the United States and Canada. Includes a chapter on game and wild fowl. $8.95, perfect bound 8½ x 11

Wild Foods of the Desert, for the hunter, backpacker, camper, prospector and gourmet cook. Discover the cornucopia of wild foods of the Southwest. $7.95 spiral

Wild Wines, one hundred wines to make from wild fruits and berries without expensive equipment or harmful chemicals. $4.95 spiral

Also:
The All Natural Brown Baggers Cookbook, $5.95
The All Natural Soup Cookbook, $5.95
The All Natural Salad Cookbook, $5.95
The All Natural Cookie Cookbook, $5.95
The All Natural Seed & Grain Cookbook, $6.95
Sack it & Pack it, $6.95
Pita Breads and Pocket Filling, $5.95
Gourmet Gifts from the Kitchen, $5.95
The Old Fashioned Confectioners Handbook, $7.95

Available through:

Darcy Williamson	or	**Maverick Publications**
P O Box 1528 • McCall, ID 83638		Drawer 5007 • Bend, OR 97708